THE ART
OF
CONTROLLING
REALITY

KSENIA MENSHIKOVA

More about Menshikova School:

Copyright © 2023 Ksenia Menshikova
English Translation Copyright © 2023 STUDIO LABYRINTH
Sp. z o.o., Poland
All rights reserved.

ISBN: 9798866642434

CONTENTS

Something like a preface	5
How to become a mage	16
Teacher	28
People	31
Money	40
Society	44
Time	46
External memory	55
Information	61
Energy	63
Informational data bank	66
Goals	69
Movement towards the goal	71
Consciousness	74
Worlds and reality	81
Reality	85
Illusion	88
Will	93
Fate	95
Karma	100
Calling	107
Events	111
Ritual	115
Bloodline and ancestry	119
Death	127
Word	134
Literature	138
World of illusions	142
Saviors and prophets	147
How to learn	150

SOMETHING LIKE A PREFACE...

Throughout the ages, people have sought to control the circumstances of their lives. They did not want to be dependent on their suddenness and unpredictability. They wanted, if not to create their circumstances, then at least to be able to foresee them. This is why "magic" as a concept, as the art and skill of controlling reality, is so attractive to men and women whose ambitions are high enough not to be satisfied with their reality.

You, too, don't want to be dependent on circumstances and would want them to change at will. You want to control your own reality. That is why you are reading this book.

"Magic" is such a fascinating word - it means omnipotence and knowledge. Magic as the art of controlling reality. Magic as an inexhaustible storehouse of knowledge. And all for what? So that you can satisfy your ambitions, your passions, your pride.

Are you suggesting it's bad? It's nothing like that! It's beautiful.

It is because of people like you that magic will always exist. It is people like you who have moved the world forward and set it on the path of progress. It is people like you who are always dissatisfied with what they have, and always want more. And that is beautiful too!

But before the ambitious and crazy pioneers turned from humans to mages, their consciousness went on a grandiose journey. Therefore, we strongly advise you to think twice before reading this book.

These days, you won't come across such science as magic. There are no research institutes that work on developing witchcraft and occultism best practices. No textbooks on probabilistic magic and Chaos magic are written, there are no Departments of Magic and Witchcraft in universities, and students do not pass laboratory exams or write term papers on the subjects of "applied magic" or "domestic witchcraft". None of this exists.

You are forced to wade through the darkness and blindly, by touch, take whatever literature you can find if it seems like it may meet your needs in some way or another. You live in a world of dreams and fiction, you try to find a mentor, but all you find is fools.

Some, having reached the halfway point, become embittered. Having accumulated some baggage of knowledge, they decide that they have risen above many - and begin to regress. Do you know why?

Because everything is an illusion, a dream, a fantasy. Both your power, and your own idea of it.

You can gain knowledge, learn a lot of spells and rituals, and it will all just be dust and an illusion. But as long as you believe in it, it is your reality. And if there are other people who believe the same things as you, it becomes your common reality.

Do you get it? Reality is created by believing in reality. If there is no faith, there is no reality. But fortunately for you, that's not the case.

All people believe in something, that's the way human beings are. And as long as there is faith, magic will live on.

Magic is a universal system of knowledge for controlling reality. Faith determines your place in the system of magical hierarchy: if you believe that you depend on reality, you are just a human being; if you believe that reality depends on you, then you will soon be able to become a mage.

But don't think that just believing in magic is enough to instantly realize yourself a mage. Ha, if only it were that simple...

Magic is above all, knowledge. A man who has knowledge but no faith is akin to a dusty book on a godforsaken shelf. A man who has faith but no knowledge is a gullible adept of the myriads of cults that are out there.

Faith is above all the power that leads you in the direction of knowledge. Only power combined with knowledge together, makes magic.

The acquisition of power and knowledge must be gradual and necessarily simultaneous. It does not matter when you started this path - 1000 years ago or yesterday - you are already on it. He who follows the path of magic will never swerve from it. He simply won't be able to.

They say that mafia members retire at the cemetery. It's even worse with magic - even a graveyard can't save you from it.[1]

So, have you changed your mind yet?

Well, well, well. Then let's move on.

The fundamental law of movement along the magical path lies in the hierarchical system, which is determined by the quantitative and qualitative characteristics of accumulated and mastered knowledge plus accumulated and mastered power.

Pay attention: knowledge and powers should be not only accumulated, but also applied, i.e. put into circulation. If you got a result on the First Circle, go to the Second Circle. If you didn't get it, start all over again. There is no liberalism here: once you pledge, don't hedge.

If you want a quiet fate, don't even go down that road. Mages have no fate at all. Their path is an eternal, endless search for knowledge and power, an endless process of their accumulation and transformation. That is why mages, as well as their science and art - magic - create this

---

[1] What an interesting observation: the word magic (Magia) is different from mafia by just one letter - there's got to be some sacred meaning in that...

world. While everyone else is only enjoying the results of this activity.

If you have begun following the path of magic, forget everything that was ever valuable and meaningful to you before - these are the illusions of the previous reality.

The hierarchy of mages, as already mentioned, depends on the results they have achieved in mastering powers and knowledge of each circle. The higher your level, the better you can control the lower circle, but the more you depend on the higher one. You have learnt to control sensations and emotions, but at the same time your dependence on the observance of the Laws of the next, higher order becomes stronger and more obvious. And it takes you by surprise.

The most important problem for all aspiring mages is determining their place in the rigid magical hierarchy. There are no diplomas or certificates here, and everyone has to determine the level of his power as it is.

If you overestimate your knowledge and power, you get a slap on the head; if you underestimate it, you get no result.
If you haven't received an ancestral gift, or if fate has not given you a mentor, but if your stubbornness however is so great that you want to become a mage at all costs, you must prepare yourself to start from the very bottom, from the most primitive work. To achieve great results, you must be ruthless with yourself.

And once you have achieved your success, you will have to develop the ability to maintain it. Thus, by defending

yourself against the attacks of others like you, you will have to learn to attack. As well as to be ruthless - not only to yourself, but also toothers.

So, what about mercy and humanity? Very possibly – but only when it benefits you. Alas, these are the realities of the journey.

In order to capture the achieved results, you will have to repeatedly learn how to achieve them under changing external and internal circumstances. The fact is that any successful practice works in the mage's mind only once. You will find out why later. Just take this axiom as a given: you will never be able to repeat the same ritual, brew the same potion, read the same spell and get the same result. So, you must repeat over and over again, a hundred times, a thousand times - and gain experience.

People are the most important source of knowledge for a mage. They are fickle creatures, unpredictable at first glance, and all so different. But you must get to know them as you know yourself, find the commonality between them all.

But that is not enough.

Start learning from getting to understand your own self. If you understand how your mind works, you will also understand how the minds of others work. If you learn to influence and change yourself, you will learn to influence and change the minds of others.

All stories of great victories in this world have a common thread: most of those who have risen to the top and got

their handful of successes are adepts of the fine art of controlling others. They are masters of understanding the nature of their strengths and weaknesses, their passions and ambitions.

But you cannot achieve this unless you study yourself thoroughly, unless you take yourself apart, down to the cell level, down to the molecule, down to the elementary particle, and ultimately, down to the light.

You can read and re-read piles of literature on the art of management (or control), attend seminars and study for an MBA, join any sect or school, but this will not bring you even one iota closer to your goal, because knowledge without power is empty, and power without knowledge is stupid and primitive. If you do not know yourself, books and studies will only deepen your own ignorance of the subject.

What will be written in this book has never been written before, as the disclosure of such knowledge has always been considered forbidden, closed off to the laymen. A mage is used to either search for answers to all his questions himself or receive knowledge from his mentor, or ancestor. This has always been the case, since the number of magical knowledge holders relative to the rest of the population had to remain unchanged in order to maintain balance. This has always been the case indeed, but only up until recently.

Not so long ago something happened that led to a distortion in the informational processes management system of the world.
The thing is that the whole informational system was

based on the postulate that magic was a constant value, meanwhile, the population was constantly growing. Therefore, only a few people were able to get into magic orders (closed associations of information carriers), and those who did were faced with so many obstacles that by the 10th-12th incarnation a mage could only but approach the information space, entering it would be impossible…

All gates were jealously guarded, but hacker-minded individuals like you don't sit still. Information was leaked, which luckily, when getting into the immature consciousness of common folk, did not find its application. But at the same time, alas, it gave rise to many problems.

Those who approached the entrance were swept away by a flood of information, generously diluted by the natural human desire to quickly improve their financial situation. Numerous gurus, schools and academies began to train all those who wished to acquire sacred knowledge. The result, as you realize, was exactly the opposite.

For every action, there is a reaction. The more prohibitions were put in front of the seekers, the more they wanted to break them. And as a result, those who really should have come were pushed a few laps back.

So, the world equilibrium began to collapse: the amount of real power steadily decreased. And this could not be allowed - everything has a meaning and purpose. Including the amount of magic present in the world.

Because mages are conduits of power. If the balance of

forces is disturbed or magic is not channeled in the proper volume, then all the processes going on here can simply get out of control.

Economic disasters, wars, national calamities - do you think it's all accidental? Ha, as if. The system needs to be rebooted periodically, especially when it starts to glitch.

Once the system starts gaining momentum again, the contract that you've signed at the beginning of your strange life suddenly stops working. All your dubious achievements - money, power, career and other human pleasures - suddenly cease to be valuable, and the values you've been upholding suddenly turn out to be rubbish. Clearly, you have to start all over again.

This is if you are a human being. But if you are a mage - at the moment when the operating system is rebooting, you write your own program, build it into the global informational space and then start living in a completely new reality. Realities, to be exact.

The system itself will keep rebooting until the world's magical balance is restored.

All mages are, in essence, loners. But the influence we exert on the common global informational space however, is joint. And here, whether you want it or not, you'll have to negotiate. To find a consensus, so to speak.

And it is precisely mages who make this process happen. It's just a job, but if it isn't done, the outcome can be very sad.
Some people think it is easier just to tear everything

down to hell and recreate a new civilization, a new world. This has been done many times before, and there are those who actually would prefer this method. But the balance of forces in the newly created worlds and, strangely enough, in the worlds preserved in other realms, will be completely different.

That's what we're trying to avoid. There are two reasons for that.

Firstly, we like this world, despite everything, we like it a lot. We like to watch it grow and mature, we like to watch people love each other and punch each other in the face, we like the way they try to make their children perfectly happy without having the slightest idea of what happiness or perfection actually are.

The second reason, however, you'll learn a little later.

Breaking everything would be the easiest thing to do. And for us, it's important to fix the situation. But for this we will need people who will walk this difficult but very interesting path with us, and together with us will restore world harmony.

Build up your power, build up your knowledge, and we'll go together. We need you, because we need those who seek and want. We need those who are ready to learn and make mistakes, those who want to grow out of their human onesies to fit the magic cloak. We need those who will continue our work.

We will search for you until we find you. We'll bring you all together. But don't be fooled by your own importance,

it doesn't exist yet. It's just that we really need this world, and all the other worlds too. And we'd like to preserve them.

You're not bored yet? You're so stubborn! Then let's move on.

The theses, concepts, pearls of wisdom and nonsense that are in this book are only elements of the description of human nature in its dynamics. But it is precisely in its fluidity that the sacred meaning of your abilities lies.

Go step by step, discover yourself step by step, get bruised, swear, burn a book in the stove, get drunk out of desperation or excitement - do whatever you want, just don't hurry.

By reading thoughtfully, repeatedly and consistently, you will eventually achieve that your knowledge of yourself will be somewhat greater than your pathetic biography, and your understanding of human nature will be broader than the profound maxim that "all men are - ...brothers" (...assholes, ...bastards, ...thieves, ...children, ...gods - emphasize it later as you see fit).

And remember: everything you do is not about the hypothetical saving of the world - let's leave the action movie hero's laurels to action movie heroes. You're doing it for yourself. You do it for your own egoistic belief that you can control your life.

HOW TO BECOME A MAGE

The best way to become a mage is to be born one. Who your mom and dad are, of course, carries a significance. They can provide you with an additional source of power, which will be written about later, but they cannot provide you with knowledge.

Some of those who have received powers by birthright consider it divine providence. They grew up with a deep conviction (alas, erroneous, as practice shows) of their own unquestionable superiority. They believe that power, just like the lack of it, comes from God and therefore they treat everyone else as mediocre.

The first time you come into contact with them, you may feel confused or even inadequate. But do not despair. Practice shows that dealing with them is easy, because a power that has not been applied nor confirmed by knowledge is like having sex by correspondence - the technique is perfected only in theory.

Knowledge builds up over thousands of years. A mage's knowledge has nothing to do with school or university-like rote learning. The knowledge of a mage is formed in the realm of experience and the laws of causation.

And it does not matter what language you are able to think in or how many languages you are able to express your thoughts in.... Well, let these dubious syllogisms be called "thoughts" for the time being. It doesn't matter.

Magical knowledge is pure knowledge that is universal for all nationalities, cultures and political movements. For magic does not depend on all these ephemeral factors. They, however, are very much dependent on it.

Many of us have been accumulating and polishing this knowledge for more than a hundred years (and some of us for more than a thousand). Quantity turns to quality, and then practice becomes Knowledge.

Everyone started with practice, some earlier, some later, but everyone started with practice. Some looked at the stars for a long time and thought that surely we are not alone in the Universe. Some, observing people, were puzzled by the unoriginal thought of why they, who are supposedly created in the image and likeness, so to speak, had so many horrible characteristics. And some, on the contrary, like Prometheus, who suddenly fell in love with people and decided to pass on some of their magical knowledge just because.

But don't wait for a silver spoon - there will be no free rides.
You will learn how to free your consciousness and how best to go from thinking like a human being to thinking like a mage. Many of us have not even had that. If it were not for extraordinary circumstances, you would not have even a fraction of what you will have going forward. But you will have to make the journey yourself, so go and pack your suitcase with your experiences and achievements.

If you happen to find a teacher along the way, you can count yourself as very lucky. The teacher will not teach

you practice, but he will explain the principle. He will not give you ready-made formulas, but he will teach you how to make them. He will not guide you through a complex hierarchy of mages, but he will explain to you how that hierarchy is structured.

He will teach you to distinguish between enemies and friends - or rather, he will explain to you that neither enemies nor friends really exist. There are only people who *think* they are your friends and people who *think* they are your enemies. As long as they think so, you can rely on them, or, on the contrary, you should be wary of them. If tomorrow circumstances change and your friends suddenly stop being friends and your enemies change their priorities in life, then they will cease being who they were before. And this will only happen if you stop thinking that you have enemies and friends.

You are a loner. You have always been a loner, and your enemies and friends are an illusion created by your own unspoken agreement with all others who are taking part in this illusion. As long as you believe in this illusion, you are its slave. You live according to the laws of illusion, and it is no longer you who rules reality, but it's the reality that is ruling you. When you realize that you are always alone in your illusion, you can get rid of it forever.

The first step on the path of magic is liberation from illusions.

Illusions are very beneficial to those who try to shape your life. How is an illusion constructed? Very simple.

First, an idea must be created. Any idea: there is a god,

there is no god, our main value is wealth, patriotism, national idea, monarchy, anarchy, law and order - anything. Then we take a natural human need to eat, drink, reproduce - that is, to survive. The need is always supported by emotion, and the strongest human emotion is fear. Fear of death, physical death. Emotion is energy, and the idea is information. The more people are involved in an idea, the more energy is used to support that idea. A certain new element forms as a result. That new element is the energy-informational space of people who are involved in this idea and who have emotions about it. It can be called a shell. And it is impossible for a mere mortal to go beyond the boundaries of this shell, since just approaching its boundaries can cause such terror and fear that the person's mind turns hollow and his will, deactivated.

Further, this shell contains other software which, firstly, can only function in this shell (operating system) and, secondly, that acts as its amplifier. A closed circle. But a little human, forced to live in this space with its created informational laws, thinks that this is his real life, thereby …creating an illusion for himself.

A lot of energy and vitality is spent on maintaining illusions. You strive for the goals prescribed to you by the illusion: to finish school, to get into a university, to get married, to have children, to build a career, to retire. And finally, to die, preferably a "natural" death, and if possible, to do so quickly and without suffering. And all just to stay within the framework of the created shell.

The harm of the illusion is that all these prescribed goals are not really goals at all. They're tools. Tools to achieve

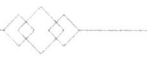

real goals. But people don't know this - the goals are substituted for the tools on purpose.

The true goal for a mage is to accumulate and preserve knowledge, to build up power.

For what? Exclusively so that all the tools you have developed for this purpose are not left behind in the world of illusions after your death, but follow you as your experience, your accumulated information.

Therefore, illusions must first be gotten rid of.

Just realizing the illusory nature of this world is not enough.
You have to feel it.

Try focusing on your body first. Yes, yes, your physical body. It is clear that you do not feel your whole body. Most likely, you feel it in fragments - where you direct your attention, that is where your sensations appear. But you have to learn to feel yourself completely, every cell, every organ and all the processes that happen within your body.

This is your **first lesson, your first step. Realize yourself for who you are.** Fat, thin, small, frail, handicapped, healthy - it doesn't matter. Just the way you are.

The shape and size of the body is irrelevant. The attitude towards your body is also an illusion. This physical shell enables you to sustain life, feeds energy to your consciousness - what else is required of it?

Then, once you learn to control the illusion and perhaps build illusions yourself, you will be able to change the appearance of your body according to your wishes. But by then you won't want to do that anymore. Because you won't care what it looks like, as long as it works.

Many mages, even women, choose to like 60–70-year-olds, although they can make themselves look any age they want. It is simply convenient that way and does not cause a hormonal release neither in the owner of the body, nor in the individuals who happen to contemplate it.

Thus, step two: take care of your body. It should be giving you a lot of energy, enough to make your consciousness work for you, not against you.

You must study your body thoroughly, its strengths and weaknesses. Later you will learn to study all aspects of your psyche just as thoroughly, but you must start somewhere, and the body is the best place for this.

Learn to turn your weaknesses into strengths, and to multiply your strengths. Each of your weaknesses, deficiencies, disabilities and injuries is your potential power: there are two sides to every coin, and there are two edges to every sword.

If nature has deprived you of some sensory function (hearing, sight, touch, smell, whatever), then you will have something that greatly compensates for this deficiency. Discover it and develop it - make it your most important tool for learning about yourself and about the illusion... pardon me, I mean the reality.

If you do this, you will be able to regulate the activity of your physiological system with a single thought. Start small by exploring your body's capabilities.

As soon as you learn to control your physical processes and develop your sensory channels to the point of being able to read information on the sensory level, **you will enter the First Circle** - the circle of psychic perception of information.

Are you expecting congratulations? There won't be any. Because now, if you don't keep going, you're going to drown in a flood of sensations and devour your own self. 90% of psychics end up this way, just so you know.

The flow of signals from the outside world becomes so great that the psychic's consciousness is simply unable to digest them. Hallucinations, hypersensitivity, voices and other unfamiliar and unpleasant things throw the already unstable system out of balance, and the poor psychics are faced with only two paths: either to develop their consciousness further, or to drown out this flow with alcohol, drugs and other things that are of little use to the body, things that disconnect a person's consciousness from all feelings and sensations.

What percentage of psychics actually follow the path of evolution do you think? Exactly, extremely few. The easiest way is to suppress, eliminate sensations, so that they do not destroy the illusion that you have so carefully created.

You too will have to go through a state of heightened sensitivity and figure it out, i.e. make it habitual for

yourself.

You have just entered the First Circle, but you have not passed it. You must develop a whole system of definitions of your own sensations, develop your body-oriented consciousness to the level of reading not only yourself but also others. Intuition will have to become your most important sense: don't believe your eyes, don't believe your ears, nor your tongue. It happens that the tongue lies and the nose doesn't smell. Intuition is the main tool that you will take with you to the **Second Circle**, it is your sixth sense.

You don't believe me? Let's do a simple experiment.

Focus on the sensations at the tip of your tongue. Don't let go of the focus for three minutes. That's all.

The new taste that you got as a result of this concentration has nothing to do with the actual change in your mouth: you ate nothing sour, nor spicy, nor salty, nor sweet. But the taste has really changed. Meaning that you can actually feel it.

But does it have anything to do with reality, or is it just a figment of the imagination, which has nevertheless produced, strangely enough, results in the physical world? What difference does it make whether it is a fantasy, illusion, or maya, if it helps you to acquire knowledge, power and results. This means that it is just a tool.

It is necessary to work with sensations, to recognize them and, of course, to evoke them at will. It is an important

tool for any mage to adjust his sensations to the task he sets for himself.

But that's not the main instrument. The most important tool is the feeling of one's own individuality. We will come to know it much later, but first, it is a feeling. This is the state all illusions are built around. Illusions change endlessly, but this state remains unchanged. **It is the state of "I Am As I Am".**

All adepts of spiritual practices strive to achieve it - whether intuitively or by guidance - mistakenly believing that this is the chief goal of spiritual growth. But no, that is a tool as well. However, it is an important one. This is the measure, according to which we determine the quality of the created illusion... sorry, I mean reality.

Close your eyes and concentrate on your mortal body. There is a vertical axis inside your body. It goes from top to bottom: from infinity to infinity. Get in touch with it, enter it. Feel the space around you expanding, the feeling of your body changing. Say to yourself: "I Am As I Am". Become aware of the changes that are taking place within you.

This is the next step, an important one. Very important. Repeat this practice until you realize: **I Am As I Am.** And that's it. Illusions don't matter. Other people's opinion of you doesn't matter. Your opinion of them doesn't matter either. What is needed is pure information about yourself, communicated through sensations.

Enter this state as often as possible. The state of the awareness of one's own self without any illusions or

pretenses. Without humiliation and self-abasement (oh no, I am so untalented and incapable!). And without excessive sense of pride from quick successes. Just self-awareness.

One day you will get something resembling an understanding, but in truth, it too will be an illusion slipped to you by your distorted consciousness. Keep practicing until Knowledge comes to you. As: "I just know it, that's all. "

At first you will think it is a play of the imagination, an illusion, as you used to think of it. There! This is it. But however delusional the realization may seem to you, believe me, you are already close to the truth about who you are. You will see it, and now the road will be much easier because you will know where to go.

But if you happen to think that the truth you see is in a close proximity to you, write a congratulatory card and mail it to yourself. By the time it reaches you, you will realize that you are even further from the truth than you were before. It does have this characteristic: the closer we think it is to us, the further away it is. An optical deception, so to speak.

Make it a rule to doubt absolutely everything, especially things that are absolutely obvious and understandable even to a baby. There is nothing more illusory than public knowledge or common opinion. Knowledge can only be personal, individual; only if you let it pass through you, through your consciousness.

From now on, keep your eyes and ears open and your

mouth shut. If you start telling everyone about your experiences and achievements, some people might not like it very much. And you still know too little to be able to compete with others.

With who? You'll find out later. But it's better if you find out when you're ready. Until then, listen carefully and don't say anything.

Study yourself, form your own attitude towards reality through the prism of **"I Am As I Am"**. And keep quiet.

TEACHER

At the beginning of the journey, everyone needs the support of a teacher - a guru, a mentor, a master, and a drill sergeant. This means that you have to learn to listen and to memorize.

All your skills of acquiring knowledge in schools and universities are worthless, because there are no teachers there. They are educators, instructors. A real teacher is someone you would trust with your life for the knowledge he or she will give you.

Find your teacher. You need him. It is better if it is a human being - that way you will understand him better.

Never look for a world-renowned, recognized or popular mage as a teacher. They are usually only concerned with their own image and fees. This is where their interests (and, alas, their opportunities) end.

Your attitude towards him can be whatever you like - love him, hate him, honor him, adore him - that is your problem. As long as he gives you knowledge and helps you gain power, he is your teacher. Whatever delusional assignments he puts in front of you, you will execute them. Once you have your own students (gods forbid!), you will be giving them an even harder time, rest assured.

You must learn to separate grain from the chaff, to learn to filter information, let it pass through your consciousness and... gain experience. Your teacher will

show you the essence, the principles of practices, rituals and so on, but you will have to do them yourself. And after you have made a lot of mistakes (not before), he will explain to you the essence of those mistakes.

You must therefore learn to ask questions. The teacher will only answer a question that already contains part of the answer. This will show him first of all that you know what you are talking about and why you are asking.

Your teacher has something that you do not have, but seek. And that is: knowledge and experience. It doesn't matter how he achieved it or how many centuries he has nurtured his knowledge for, the most important thing is that he has it. And you will do anything to get this knowledge in a much shorter period of time. If you must pay, pay. If you must do his dirty work for him, you'll do it as long as you're an apprentice. Pure servility and running around with your hair on fire is quite normal in apprenticeship, we all went through it. And we did it willingly and brilliantly.

But! If you are forced to bow, bow as low as you can. And remember that feeling forever.

You'll also learn to keep your rage in check. This skill - keeping your emotions in check - will come in very handy later, when you need to collect all power for a decisive battle (mages don't duel: you will only have a chance for one strike at best. If you miss, you're dead).

Get from your teacher all that he has. Remember, once upon a time, like you, he started at the bottom and stood on the shoulders of his teacher.

If you think that a teacher will be happy to give you his accumulated knowledge, you are very much mistaken. You will become his ulcer, his pain in the arse, his nightmare, but most importantly, you will beat what you want out of him.

But if at any point you realize that your guru begins to hinder your development, look for another one.

We also take on apprentices sometimes. If a person is worth something, we coddle them and babysit them even if it becomes unbearable and painful for all the involved, we still coddle them. But if he's not worth it, we put an end to the project. Dixi.

PEOPLE

People are the most valuable material for research and learning. Study people - all of them together and each of them separately. Study how they feel and think. Search for a system within it.

People are herd-like creatures by nature. Most of them want everything to be as good as their neighbor's. Rarely do they actually ask themselves: why do I need it?

Ask anyone: what do they aspire to? You will get a lot of platitudes: love, happiness, prosperity. Ask: why? Out of 100 answers, gods willing, one will be a good answer.

People do not think about their personal, individual goals. So, they go with the flow.

Yet those same people, with all their flaws, vices, stupidity and incompetence, are the stuff which your success as a mage depends on.

Human passions and ambitions set this world in motion. The direction of motion is set by information, and mages are the ones who hold information. But without power, without energy, there is no movement.

To study people, you must learn to become unnoticeable, inconspicuous, transparent. People will reveal their nature to you, fanning their tails and shimmering with all the colors of their primitive ambitions.

Don't stand out too much from your surroundings and don't join anyone - listen and observe wholeheartedly. Blend in, but don't stand out.

The most powerful and influential among us speak softly, quietly and very little. Speaking quietly makes others listen to you. And remember: the more you talk, the less they listen. You try to draw attention to yourself, you show emotion and.... you open up.

Important: learn to keep your cool, don't get caught up in spontaneous emotions; keep your distance. You can't know everything, so don't reveal your knowledge unnecessarily. Because at any moment you may meet someone who knows more than you. It is better to be looked at as an idiot than to risk being exposed badly.

Inconspicuousness is one of the basic rules of a mage's presence among people.

That grandpa in the plaid shirt with the quiet and gentle look who plants and transplants vegetables in his garden, who do you think he is? An unassuming retiree living out his nostalgic illusions? Maybe he is, maybe he isn't. But perhaps he planted some cabbage in his garden, and the US influence on the global financial markets has changed; perhaps he decided that there was no place for carrots in his raised bed any longer, and a small African country changed its government after a military coup; perhaps he tied up the tomatoes and some former Soviet country received another set of funds from the IMF.

He listens and observes. And who would have thought that they were in the presence of the greatest mage and

wizard, the legends of whom have been handed down by word of mouth for generations?

And this man behind the president's back - who is he? In all the official photos you can only recognize his ear (for some reason nothing else is in the frame). An accident?

And that elderly lady on the bench outside of your apartment building? She has already become part of the exterior, and your neighbor, when trying to find his way home while intoxicated, uses her presence as sort of a lighthouse that leads him to the right building. Why is she sitting there? Who is she watching? What events does she capture?

Do you know?

Therefore, step three: Explore the opportunities that other people give you. Study people, their personalities, passions, affections, opinions and values and... mold what you learn into a system.

When interacting with others, you will learn to maximize the results of the communication if you view everything through the prism of expediency. Two questions: "How beneficial is it to me?" and "How beneficial is it for him?" - shall set the record straight. Immediately and forever.

A mage never acts as he wishes. He does not want anything from the point of view of human desires. A mage acts in a way that benefits him, coming from the main goal - to accumulate power and knowledge.

They try to involve you in the emotional experience of

other people's values, other people's problems: attention everybody, the world is in a crisis! We are all facing job loss (poverty, imprisonment, divorce, pandemic, etc.), and if that's the case, we all must immediately begin to worry and suffer. If you get involved in these experiences even for a moment, then you have become like everyone else. And from that moment on, all the abovementioned problems become yours.

If you think that experiencing such problems is inevitable, do as you wish. Your reaction to external circumstances will become the essence of your life: event - reaction, situation - reaction. And the funny thing is that the reaction will be predictable: if you are told to worry about the crisis, you worry; if you are told to fight for your love, honor, career, fortune, you will unquestionably fight with all your heart.

And who is it told by? You'll find out a little later as well.

If you are involved in a system of shared, collective worries, then you are a part of society, and forget to even think about your individuality. You are a part, and therefore an easily replaceable element like any other. The society of people, this collective mind, will move you aside, exclude you, push you out, if you do not fit into the common system of worries.

So, the next step in your magical work is to acquire the ability to want without wanting. To desire without desiring. To experience an emotion without tuning into it.

If you can do that, **you have entered the Second**

Circle: controlling the force of desire.

Let go of the unnecessary fears, phobias and other nonsense that tell you what you can do (experience, feel) and what you can't. Leave only one fear in your arsenal: the fear of physical death. This fear is not the meaning of life, it is a tool like everything else. It will be your helper in all your practice, a criterion of evaluation - your flesh and bones must work, work and work.

Just beware lest that this fear embedded in your biology doesn't become a host for other fears that can so cleverly come disguised as an instinct of self-preservation.

Learn to separate natural fears from implanted fears. This skill will come in handy later on when you learn to separate your own goals from extraneous ones.

You live among people, take that as it is. By studying each person individually and people as a whole, you will develop a common understanding of all their passions and desires. You will understand the mechanisms by which they arise. By realizing this, you will gain access to another tool and an infinite resource: human energy.

But this will happen if there are no hang-ups, fears and passions left within you, no attachments to your own past, neither hopes for a hypothetical future.

Free yourself from illusions about having friends, enemies, love, commitments to others, passionate attraction - a mage has none of these things. They are social roles wrapped in brightly colored packages of feelings that you mistake for your values.

Today you have your friends, your loved one, your wife (husband) and you enjoy and revel in the happiness of your attachment. But tomorrow your friend betrays you, or your loved one leaves you, or your husband hops into bed with another woman - and you begin to suffer.

Your hard-earned power is spent on suffering. Only because you depend on the way other people treat you.

Think about it: your power is at the mercy of others. There's no need to talk about magic if you willingly put the levers of your life into someone else's hands.

Any connection, passion, trust, any emotional experience should strengthen you in the here and now. If the connection breaks, your energy, your power, must remain with you.

If you let yourself get hurt, you have made a huge setback and will have to start all over again in many ways.

Get rid of the illusion that people around you belong to you in some or any way. Circumstances will change and they will screw you, dump you, betray you, and you find yourself dependent from this perspective because you are under the illusion that you can control another person's feelings.

This skill of managing other people's feelings and aspirations are as far away from you as the moon. You must first learn to manage your own feelings.

Take a close look at your surroundings in the "here and now". Recognize how each connection strengthens you or, on the contrary, makes you weaker. Take a critical look at all your illusions and become conscious of them.

We only go for a long-term connection when it provides us with power.

If it's love that gives us power - long live love!

If work helps you to fulfill your ambitions or creativity - yay!

Friends have our backs - we are grateful to them today.

But always remember that love, work and friendship can end at any time due to circumstances that are beyond your control.

The mage is free from attachments, passions and obligations. The mage interacts with others only when it is to his advantage.

The only person you can trust at all times and under all circumstances is your own self.

The man who plays alone never loses.

He who is responsible for others, pays their bills.

If we realize that a person (job, system) is trying (!) to get more from us than we are prepared to give, we tear up those contacts ruthlessly. And we learn an additional lesson and gain another experience about our own imperfection.

Learn to build relationships with people in such a way that no one would ever even think that they could bite a piece of you for free.

So never give people any information about yourself that they can use against you. "We cannot foresee how our words will come back to us"... The thinking process of a mage is different from that of all other people, because he isn't only able to instantly calculate such consequences, but he simply knows them.

If the circumstances are such that you have to entrust someone with information about yourself, entrust only part of it. As long as people do not know everything about you, they will depend on you. Otherwise, you will be the one dependent on them.

Therefore, you should not burden people with your excessive trust.

People are only good at keeping secrets they don't know.

Friends who come into your life after you have already taken up the path of a mage, should be of special suspicion to you. All we need is as many allies as possible.

An enormous value to a mage are people who consider themselves our enemies. They never let you relax. They force you to improve your knowledge and skill. But watch their behavior and your own actions carefully, so that their enmity does not lead you astray.

Learn to control your enemies by showing fear. It is much better if people who think you are their enemy consider you mad and cowardly rather than rational and sober.

But if you find yourself cornered and your chances of winning are doubtful, do everything you can to make the cost of the enemy's victory as high and as unreasonable as possible.

If you are punishing a wrongdoer, do it publicly. A quick and hard injection of the inevitability of punishment and payment of dues in the minds of all others will save you from wasting any further power on war.

Study human relationships, accumulate information about how things are and how things happen. Draw conclusions and free yourself from attachments.

By studying and learning about human society, you will learn not to stand out from it. Learn to be inconspicuous, transparent - the real power is not with those who shout loudly, but with those who tell the shouters *what* to shout.

A man who lacks the opportunity to sin considers himself righteous; a thief who lacks the opportunity to steal considers himself honest. People remain in a perpetual illusion about themselves.

Remember this and don't get caught up in other people's illusions.

MONEY

In the human world, money is the equivalent of power and intelligence. In the magical world, it's a tool for interaction with the human world.

If you see money as a tool for your main goal, that is to accumulate power and knowledge, you will have as much of it as needed in the "here and now".

Mages are not in the business of saving and hoarding - it takes a lot of energy and emotion and is as much a means of manipulating your mind as is love, passion, fear, and so on.

None of us would squander power and knowledge for the dubious pleasure of making capital for capital's sake - it is too primitive of an aspiration.

You must always know why you need this equivalent of human interaction for: and if you need a house to protect your behind, you will have the opportunity for it. And money has nothing to do with it.

People often substitute tools for goals, which is why they suffer from a lack of those very tools.

You understand that money is materialized energy. But knowing that energy is needed to bring you closer to knowledge, you will change your attitude towards this human equivalent of energy exchange.

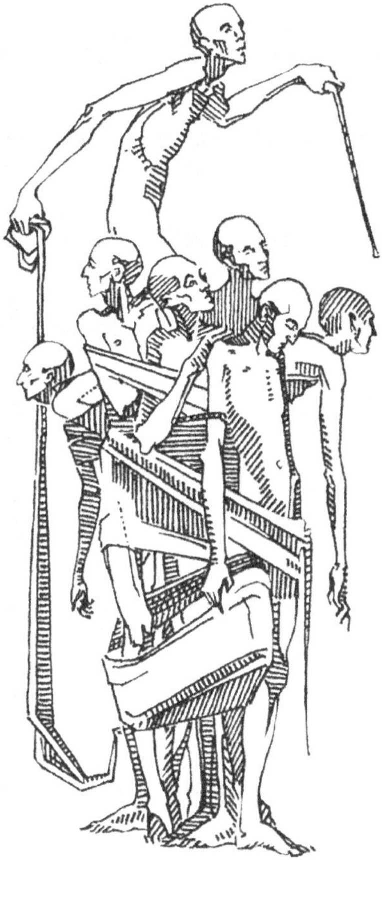

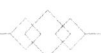

People work with and for people and use the standard levers for this - greed and fear.

Get rid of this, while working on the Second Circle and formulate for yourself the basic precepts for dealing with people.

Every human being wants to feel significant. Use this natural human desire to achieve your goals.

Meanwhile, be cynical about relationships - people love that. But be honest in your calculations. That is a must. If you got what you need from another person, pay them back: whether with money, energy, love, respect, that is, what is of value to them. An equivalent **to their value.**

The main motivation of people who accumulate money is to show their importance by having authority over others. Authority is achieved for a purpose and is as much of a tool as anything else.

If you seek authority for the sake of your own primitive desire to satisfy your own importance, you are its slave. Mages do not seek authority - it takes a lot of energy and distracts from the goal. Mage requires people with authority.

Take every opportunity for your own benefit, ask yourself: "What will I get out of this and how does it fit my goal?"

If you are faced with the choice of money or connections (reputation, opportunities), think before you choose.

Don't deal with other people's problems, observe them.

Never give advice, help, nor money to anyone unless you see benefit in it other than satisfying your sense of self-worth.

If you are given free advice, accept it. Give back by thanking or curtseying. And be sure to listen to the advice that gives you an advantage.

Never give that kind of advice yourself.

Don't do yourself what other people can do for you - be sure to manage your time.

And most importantly, free yourself from attachments.

Attachments are binding. They bind you to people, to things, to places, to relationships, to lifestyles, to behaviors - all these are expectations. You are more vulnerable and defenseless the more attachments you have. Even the most innocent relations and habits can be disastrous for those who seek themselves in the world of magic.

SOCIETY

Society is made up of people, but it has no face. The hallmark of a society is its rules of behavior, values and principles.

Your next step will be to study the society as a whole, understanding the system of hierarchy of values and principles.

Do that and you've entered the **Third Circle.** Precisely from this point on. All that used to precede this was a walk in the park, so to speak, a preparatory course.

Society manifests its attitudes through rules of behavior. Knowing these rules is not enough, you must understand what lies behind them.

You will learn the principles of society's influence on each individual, and the mechanisms for influencing people's deepest feelings through the general rules of society.

On this circle, you must be able to instantly calculate the stereotypical reaction of people to an external event. You must learn to act quickly. Knowing human nature will help you delegating your tasks to those around you and thus act even faster.

Luck comes to those who know a lot and are able to put their knowledge into practice. Mages are lucky when they want to be lucky[2].

By asking yourself the right questions ("What will I get out of it?" and "What will he get out of it?"), you will be able to get what you want through other people, while doing them a huge favor.

If you are able to rally up your team (employees, family, friends), do everything you can to make them happy by means of your tasks. Their actions to achieve your goals should fulfill their strongest ambitions and deepest desires.

People think (often wrongly, but always without doubt) that always and in everything they proceed and act only in their own interests. Do not shatter their illusions.

Your task as a mage is to make them see their own interests in yours. Then they will work on the task set by you.
Symbiosis, mutual benefit always and in everything.

But once received, the mage will always multiply it. While creating a surplus value - power and knowledge.

Remember: not everyone wants to be a mage. Some are content with just being humans. Help them to do so, and they will do anything for you in the name of their goal.

---

[2] But it is worth noting that there are some practices and stages of magical formation when it is necessary to consciously switch off the program of luck and to refuse it. Because luck is relaxing. It can easily turn on laziness of the mind. And that means death for a mage. Far or near, but always death.

TIME

It is the greatest asset a mage can have. Time is short, we are extremely limited by the time allotted to the functioning of our physical body.

Usually, such understanding comes around the age of 70-80, which marks the beginning of the most productive period in a mage's life. Each of us finds our own ways to prolong the existence of this physical incarnation, and you too will find yours.

As a rule, mages go for these three options:

1st. Find a way to prolong physical existence in real time. This is a long, painful and not always effective process, because it requires influence at the cellular, genetic level. The most successful experiments yielded results of 300 400 years, but this is still not enough, and such work takes a lot of time and energy.

2nd. To condense time to such an extent that you live 10 or even 20 years in one earth year. This is a more productive way, and that is the option we usually turn to.

3rd. Learning to preserve the accumulated knowledge from incarnation to incarnation with its instantaneous unpacking at the moment of each subsequent birth. This is called complete memory.

Some old-school mages practice periodic immersion into the state of samadhi. This method is good for preserving power and knowledge, but not for accumulating them.

All methods have their pros and cons.

We propose an integrated way of the first, second and third options: to prolong the productive use of the physical body you have, to compact the time and to preserve information.

The effectiveness of this approach, as you realize, is much greater.

This is the Fourth Circle of the path and, in fact, an integration of the previous three. The Fourth circle is time management.

So, time. This subjective substance is influenced by the mage's thoughts. That is, for all people time flows according to the face of a clock, but the mage would speed up and slow down time according to his own desire. Desires are subordinated to goals. Goals derive from the task. Task is defined by the mission.

Option one. Keep your body healthy. Feed it what it needs, but don't overfeed it. Don't let it get overweight, but don't starve it either. Anything too much can have negative consequences.

Feed the body only when necessary to maintain physical power, and only what this power asks for. To do this, you must learn to listen to it and to understand it enough to know its needs instantly (not its wants, but its needs - this is important!). This is the practice of the First Circle, and if you did not achieve this result back then, go back and work with the body.

Periodically, at least once a year, cleanse your physical body by fasting. You will be able to cleanse yourself at the cellular level and, above all, to free yourself from unnecessary information that you have taken in with bad food and liquids.

There are too many sources of negative signals around you, too many. An impressionable person like you, with all your manifested and unmanifested power, can pick up this negativity with drink and food. No matter how much we limit ourselves when we live among people, it is inevitable.

That is why mages and wise people leave the human world for deserts and caves. But you must learn to live among humans if you really want to be a mage. A real one.

Learn to regulate your well-being by the power of thought. Don't let illnesses and ailments take away your energy.

You must know how to defend yourself against external influences that are aimed at draining your power. There will be plenty of clever people who would like to feed on your energy - there are a lot of them nowadays, the lazy ones...

But the best way to protect yourself at all times and in all things, is to stay out of the area of impact. But more on that later.

Option two. Time compaction. Any mage knows that working too much is not good for you. Working hard for the benefit of someone, is not for us.

All work should yield the maximum effect in the shortest possible time. How can this be achieved?

Benefit from every of your actions. To do this, you must think before each movement about how it will benefit your chief goal of acquiring knowledge and power. Never act thoughtlessly.

Any partying, talking about nothing, may seem as nothing at first glance. But you could benefit every second of your time when interacting with other people or with yourself.

A mage's time is never free - even a dull crime story can provide a lot of useful information if you can read; sex can give you more energy if *you can feel*[3].

Determine the time of day or night when you are most productive. Forget all the dogma you have learnt from the grimoires, such as that every magical operation should be executed at an appropriate time.

A favorable arrangement of the stars may indeed strengthen you and your natural forces, but what is the use of working if they are initially at zero? And whatever you multiply by zero, well, you know what that result is....

---

[3] People tend to use sex for release. Mages use it to gain power.

Take into account the millennia of proven knowledge, but start from your own understanding of self.

Don't let circumstances affect your time. Try to do everything you can to not depend on other people: Being stuck in traffic, arriving early to a meeting and waiting, sacrificing personal time for someone else. This is inefficient and takes up valuable time. Have you read "The Tale of Lost Time"? Have you seen the movie? Check it out. The tale itself is a lie, but it contains a hint.

Your time that you waste in vain is bound to be picked up by someone else. You may even learn to collect time so carelessly lost by some duds.

Therefore, if we have to, we take the metro, we walk, we wear simple and comfortable clothes - it's easier and saves a lot of time. In your car, drowning in jewels and Cartier watches, wearing designer fashion, you are very vulnerable and limited. A mage needs freedom - everywhere and in everything.

For a mage, all this paraphernalia of "belonging", so to speak, are nothing more than tools for interacting with a certain stratum of society. Well, the one where one judges a man by his clothes. And if you treat these things as tools, you will have as many of them as you need. That said, as well as other material goods, if this is not your goal.

If you find yourself in a situation where you do have to wait, use this time wisely - gain knowledge.

Sometimes 10 minutes of patience can add up to 10 years

of extra time.

For your work, choose not only a convenient time, but also a place where you feel most comfortable. This applies to everything, from business meetings to meditation. You may be seen as someone "off their rocker", a weirdo, as someone with no sense of propriety - what do you care?

The most productive thoughts, the greatest effects will be achieved at the "right" time and in the "right" place.

And for an appetizer, the most important thing of all. If someone can do your job for you, let them do it. Your teacher, by the way, is doing just that. Do you think it's so hard for him to do that simple ritual you spent three hours on? Or do you think that stupid client you've wasted more than 40 minutes of your special life on, would be difficult for him to handle? No, of course not. But if it is possible to delegate the routine to someone else, any mage will do it gladly, quickly, and without the slightest guilty conscience... due to the lack of such.

Take this principle into account - delegate your responsibilities, your tasks: for money, for teaching or for "not in service, but in friendship" - whatever it is.

Never stick to a rigid schedule that you foolishly made the day before. Remember: plans are made to be broken.

Be flexible at all times and in all things. If circumstances change, and not by your will, you must quickly adapt to them. It can be a matter of seconds: if you are late, you lose. And losing in our business is sometimes equivalent to death.

In the end, the most flexible element becomes the controlling element in the system.

Option three. Preservation of information. Once death comes, the information in your consciousness starts to fold, to archive.

Any memory is an energy-informational construct where energy takes shape by means of information. The problem for most people is that they cannot retain their memory after death.

The reason for this is that a person's memory usually only captures what he or she has experienced emotionally or physically. Which is easier to remember: a mathematical formula or an impressive journey? That's right, if math is not your thing, it's not easy to remember, and it's almost impossible to recollect. But events filled with impressions and emotions are as easy and simple as "hello".

Information cannot be unpacked without a source of energy, sensations, and emotions. And this source is the physical body. Without it, information cannot be unpacked. In order to free yourself from such dependence, you will have to learn to separate the physical-emotional experience from information.

For example, you performed a successful ritual, achieved an effect, and felt joyfully and emotionally uplifted about it. The "action-emotion" connection is stored in your memory. The next time you need to remember the ritual itself (i.e. the sequence of actions), you will be able to do so.

You can only do this with the corresponding bodily sensation, which you can recollect through the corresponding emotion, and in no other way.

Or an example from life: you are studying for an exam with Tom Waits' music in the background. Once at the exam, you can't remember a single line until the familiar tune starts playing in your ears.

All this is called the body-oriented memory. But the trick is that in the next incarnation you will come in a completely different body, which will have a different physical and energetic structure. And without the previous carrier you will not be able to read a single byte of memory in the usual way - that is through the body and emotions. It is like trying to insert a tape record into a computer – nothing will work, you need an adapter, a converter.

This function is usually performed by magical amulets and talismans. And many colleagues have relied heavily on them in the past - but they were wrong. No, nothing happens to the amulet; it still fulfills its function. But not for you, but for someone else. In the new incarnation you are lacking a simple memory - where it was that you put it.

In order to be able to unpack all the accumulated experience from your memory, it is necessary to learn to record information separately from the body, meaning, having first separated it from emotions and sensations.

In the next incarnation, in a different body, you will live with completely different sensations and emotions. But the memory of the previous incarnation will sometimes break through to the surface. Therefore, it is not surprising that you sometimes experience strange and inexplicable sensations. This is archaic information trying to "unpack" itself on a new medium.

Is it strange to feel the weight of a two-handed sword in the moment of danger, especially if you are a small and fragile woman? And where does a preacher's eloquence come from during an exam when you can't usually put two words together?

But an unsuccessful unpacking can lead to distorted information, or even its complete loss. This is why, as a rule, people do not remember their past lives, let alone the events that took place in them.

That is why, for a mage, it is certainly better to copy information in its pure form with minimum energy where it will be preserved and won't get damaged. And, of course, on a medium that can't get lost in space and time.

And, naturally, you must develop the ability to use informational constructs for thinking, remembering and reproducing.

This is the Fourth round of work - accumulation of information in the form of formulas of cause-effect relationships and their upload to an external medium.

EXTERNAL MEMORY

The exported memory will exist even after your physical death and will retain all your knowledge, accumulated and gained through experience, acquired skills and built-up power.

But that is, if you have done everything correctly: hosting, saving, and learning ways to retrieve it.

It takes a lot of energy to create an external memory. It is rare that one person can create an external memory by himself.

You have to be a very important person in this life, worshiped by millions, to create your own personal, individual egregore - an element of the collective mind.

People will give you their love or hate, adoration or contempt - it doesn't matter, they will give you their emotion and therefore their power.

Popularity in any sphere - mages are not fond of it very much. That is why we use already created egregores, such as "hosting our site on someone else's server".

The smartest and strongest among us use the egregore of magic and the old gods for this purpose.

Firstly, in the hierarchical structure of egregores, it has always stood and will always stand above any other egregorial structures. For magic is higher than passions and has in its arsenal more knowledge and more information. This information possesses a controlling function in relation to all underlying egregores.

Further down the egregorial hierarchy you will find:

- The egregorial structures of religious denominations (4 main ones - Christianity, Islam, Buddhism, Judaism - including a bunch of additional and derivative ones that are part of them);
- The egregorial structures of countries (depending on their power and placement on the playing field) and cities;
- Egregorial structures of spontaneous formations - fashions, hobbies, other temporary short-lived formations.

Then there are very small structures, such as the egregores of organizations, families, bloodlines, etc.[4]

For any egregorial structure, such things as feelings, conscience, principles, morals and values are instruments of influence on human consciousness.

Small egregorial structures are part of the larger ones, they overlap, intertwine, feed on their ideas and thus provide a communication circuit between the larger egregorial structures.

The dominant egregore in the structure is considered to

---

[4] The egregorial structure of the world is, of course, more complex, but you can read more about it in other books by Ksenia Menshikova.

be the one that is able to absorb other egregors.

I'm presenting it in a very simplistic way. Don't try to visualize it graphically. Just grasp the principle.

The most important thing in understanding the complex hierarchy of egregorial structures is that no matter how free and advanced you seem to yourself, you ALWAYS interact with one or another egregorial structure.

They, like spiders with their web, have entangled all energy-information processes of this Planet. That is why our world is called the world of the Spider.

Egregores supply you with information through the values and beliefs, principles and morals that they instill in your consciousness. They create your reality as it is now.

Now do you understand why any reality is an illusion?

No matter which egregore you get under, you will still get information directly or indirectly related to the egregore from which you escaped. Or rather, which you tried to escape from.

All egregores are interconnected and rarely fight directly. The big ones absorb the small ones, and such hostile takeover tends to destroy one's illusory reality if a person is fully included (with all of their consciousness) into any egregorial structure.

Mages communicate with egregores, study them, learn to interact with them with maximum efficiency for themselves.

And this is the Fifth Circle of gaining power and knowledge.

Without getting hung up on principles and beliefs, without having burning desires to achieve success, money, wealth, love and fame at any cost, you have a chance to free yourself from the pathological influence of any egregore and get a chance to interact with them consciously.

Winning at any cost is not our principle at all. Our principle is to win, inexpensively[5].

From the egregorial structures we receive the information we need to fulfill the tasks in the "here and now."

There are various possible ways one can extract information about themselves from an egregorial structure, including buying it out. But to fulfill the mage's task, it would be more expedient to learn to interact with them and to organize such a communication circuit as it is needed by the mage himself.

You can create an external memory in any of the egregores, but where is the guarantee that in the next incarnation your carrier will not be absorbed by a stronger and more powerful egregore? There is no guarantee, especially since something like that happens

---

[5] Thanks to Sir Joughin Halley for this thesis. We have taken it into consideration. Our respect.

all the time.

Suppose you had retained your memory in some magical Order for which you had worked all your life, but the limitations of your consciousness did not allow you to consider that this Order will not exist forever. When you come to your next incarnation, in about 300 years or so, you will be born into a completely Catholic family, which, from birth, drills the immutable tenets of Catholicism right into your brain.

Your resistance is desperate from the cradle, and parents and society are crushed by the incomprehensible child that is growing up in their family.

And your consciousness will be actively trying to find information that it has set aside for itself, not knowing that it has long been chewed up, digested and spit out by the chaps from the Vatican.

Were you born in the middle of Russia, but you are irresistibly drawn to Tibet? Or to Africa? Draw your conclusions.

Do you think the missionary endeavors of the 19th and 20th centuries were in vain? That's right.

It is good if your power and knowledge that you've accumulated in the past incarnation was enough to manifest on this Earth, which you are already familiar with, and not on some other planet. Some people must come into conflict with the egregorial structure of the State, not realizing the true, deepest reason for it until a certain moment.

And once having understood it, to leave the apparently prosperous country for another, where "normal people" in principle should not live, so to speak.

Another thing is that someone who awakens a mage within him is not quite human any longer.

Mages took their egregorial structure into the supra-egregorial realm primarily by freeing themselves from human passions and vices.

Human imperfection, emotional attachments are a tool of influence on human consciousness used by any existing egregore.

We have freed ourselves from attachments and desires and have been able to transcend the human hive mind. It is precisely in our personal egregore, in our each individual Order, is where we keep our sites, pages and portals (depending on who made how many), storing there all of our accumulated information in the form of knowledge.

INFORMATION

Is the greatest asset in this world. Only because it's very difficult to create.

That stream of signals that bombards you from the outside world is not information quite yet.

Rumors, gossip, stock market reports, news, tips, secrets - this is not information either. It's insights.

It will become information only once all this flow is used in real action. That is, it will enter the mage's consciousness and turn into a deed.

In order for an act to take place, there must be an energetic carrier to perform the act. That is the human body.

For a mage, information is the quintessence of energy and the flow of signals, which turns into the experience of doing (or non-doing, which is essentially the same thing).

Only when you realize what practical applications can be made of the insights that you have gained, can you consider that you have gained information.

Learn to get insights in every possible way, check and double-check it, distill it and shape it into information.

Most of the insights have no immediate practical

application in the "here and now", but once acquired, it never leaves our consciousness.

If you are faced with a task and your consciousness is feverishly trying to convert insights into information, you can safely put the problem out of your mind. Your subconscious will keep working on it, and when it is ready, the results and conclusions will pop up in your head.

And that is information. A ready-made solution for practical application.

Everything you have ever heard, seen, touched, smelled or vaguely guessed is in your memory. It is important to be able to retrieve this entire stream at the right moment from your memory.

So develop your memory, your observation and most importantly, your attention.

Attention is mage's most important tool.

It is not without reason that one of the most important tenets of any magical practice says: **"Where there is attention, there is energy"**.

ENERGY

Any work, much less in magic, requires power. Energy is power. It is stupid, mindless, subtle, high, low, it is just power.

At all times, mages have sought a source of power as energy.

There are "right" places on this planet where the energy release is strong enough, but there are also places that take energy away.

The first, work on the "exit", and are necessary for the mage to accumulate force, and the second, work on the "entry", and are necessary for the discharge of negativity and for cleansing.

Explore such places on the planet, they will help you in emergencies.

The energy of this Earth is everywhere, you just have to learn to receive it.

Concentrate your attention on your feet. Feel their volume and heaviness. As soon as the sensation reaches its limit, pull your attention down as far as you can. At some point you will feel a return. A stream of force will start flowing into your feet, which you have buried in the Earth via your concentrated attention.

Work with this source until you learn to switch it on

instantly, just by centering on the feeling of your soles.

As soon as you feel this flow, pull it up to run through your whole body. Fill every cell of your body with force.

At first you will feel lapses and unevenness. Keep working and practicing until you have a completely homogeneous feeling throughout your body. You and Earth are one.

You must feel her deep, slow breath. You must get into resonance with it.

We don't know how long it will take you to do this practice: it may switch on immediately, or it may take years before you feel any semblance to the sensation you want.

How long will your stubbornness and persistence last? That will be up to you.

Once the power embraces you completely, you will feel that there is no limit to your consciousness, just as there is no limit to your possibilities. Your consciousness will rush upwards into the common informational space.

The maximum effect of this practice can be achieved in nature or in places of power.

But most of us live in crowded areas, and we've learnt to use them as a source of additional force. No, it's not about primitive vampirism.

Every person is a unicum, a treasure trove of

possibilities, a completely unique talent. If you can help them to reveal it, they will give you a lot of energy - good, clean, positive, directed, already structured energy.

It will go directly to your target, your cause.

The ability to take energy from the Earth and the surrounding world, the ability to pull it up at once and to concentrate it within yourself is an indicator of a mage's personal power.

When you learn to control your energy, you will be given access to the general informational bank.

INFORMATIONAL DATA BANK

The energy that you have managed to pull through your whole body, through all levels of your consciousness, is able to take you to the Common Informational Space.

And if you don't find information in its purest form in the outside world, you shall find it here. It is the quintessence of every possible variation of knowledge and experience that has been experienced by all the people who have come and gone before you and with you. It is absolute information.

This databank contains all variants of all events that can happen.

Are you closer to your goal? Isn't that what you wanted: to control circumstances, probabilities, events? This is another illusion that all novice mages have stumbled over.

Information that you manage to grasp in the Common Information Space, will have to be dragged through your consciousness by you and materialized on the physical plane.

Focus on the sensation of the Earth current. Let it flow with all its power through your mind and body. Become part of this current. Carry it upwards with your attention until you reach a crystal clear, unrestricted space. You will not confuse it with anything. It is a space of pure, absolute information.

If you've had situations in your life where you've had insights and unique insightful solutions come out of nowhere, then you've been there before and you know what we're talking about.

But only the power of your intention and enough energy can bring you into this space and fit your consciousness into this continuous flow of information.

This space can only be reached by a pure and unclouded consciousness, free from egregorial distortions and its own limitations.

The information of your consciousness combined with energy creates the energy-informational space of your individuality. It is this information that is the foundation for the formation of reality.

If you yourself, your consciousness, have distortions, little hooks - passions, fears and hang-ups on emotions, karmic distortions, attachments and other defects - you will be able to implement only those situations that are a mirror image of your distorted consciousness.

The Common Informational Space is located above the egregorial space, permeating it completely. Egregorial structures act as a filter that gives the information a certain form.

The mage is able to combine these two currents - energy and information - in his consciousness, passing them through the necessary egregorial structures, forming in his inner world the prerequisites for the creation of a situation. And embody them in physical reality.

In order for the intention of the mage to be manifested in the form of events and situations, he must never lose sight of the Main Goal.

GOALS

In the case of an ordinary person, the behavior of the average person changes, as a rule, under the influence of circumstances. A mage has only one goal, and it never changes.

A mage may have tasks to accomplish in the "here and now," but he will always remember his goal.

The true goal for a mage is to accumulate power and knowledge. All the rest are derivatives and tools, tasks and questions to be solved in order to achieve the goal.

If you are not clear about the direction you are going, you will be given it. But there is no guarantee that you will be Informed of it.

Don't expect to meet people with whom you have common goals in life and forever. It's an illusion.

You may have common problems, common issues, common interests, common tasks. But not goals.

People's goals intersect at certain points in space and time.

People who live within a single plane believe that their life is a straight line made up of dots. Therefore, they are unable to allow into their lives the thought that the direction of another person's movement can take them in the exact opposite direction at any moment, even though in the physical world you may be walking together side by side.

Mages live within space and have no illusions about the path of others traveling in their laid out orbits.

You have the right to change your direction of travel if your primary goal requires it. Your companions do too, by the way.

You'll meet people along the way that you're comfortable with. But it's only temporary. You may be followed by admirers and disciples. But that too is temporary.

If you know that you are always alone on your path, you will never be disappointed or lose your power while on it.

Power will give you freedom. Knowledge will help you keep that freedom.

Very honestly: at the moment we have the same goals - you want knowledge, we want the balance of the world - that is our task. Once the world is in order, it is likely that our goals will not be the same. And that is normal.

The acquisition of power and knowledge - a goal that sounds the same for all those who follow the path of magic - is in fact deeply individual for each one of us.

Everyone chooses their own strategy and tactics; everyone decides HOW to move towards their goal.

MOVEMENT TOWARDS THE GOAL

The pursuit of goals is a great art. There is a lot of literature on this topic, seminars and other sources of information.

You are taught to set goals "correctly", to formulate them "correctly" and to have a "correct" attitude towards your goals.

It's okay that your teachers and mentors are usually people who have no idea how to achieve goals in real life. They usually have not achieved anything good themselves.

Not without reason there is such a saying among mages: "He who knows how to do - does; he who does not know how to do - teaches; he who does not know how to teach – teaches the one who teaches".

The most important thing in the process of achieving a goal is to be able to stop in time.

Are you surprised? But nothing is surprising. And you will probably remember it yourself, if you take a minute to reflect on your journey through life.

Living in a 2D world, you set the same 2D goals for your life and build the same straight paths towards them.

There's you, there's the target, and there's a straight line between them. That's it. Then all you have to do is to get up and run at full speed towards your goal, without taking your eyes off the road or looking around. Because there's a runner just like you running next to you. And if you don't win, someone else will.

This is a perfectly normal approach that may have worked for you on more than one occasion. But probably not the one you had in mind when you were pursuing some purpose.

The problem is, that even this limited reality has at least three dimensions, not to mention that the other worlds that pervade it are more multidimensional than you can imagine with your flat vision and thinking.

By crossing a parallel space, you can shorten the path to your goal many, many times over. And while your rival is panting to cover the distance, you can "cut the corner" and reach your goal by crossing space at the same moment when you started moving, and sometimes even earlier.

But to do this, you must be able to stop, interrupting the inertial motion at the moment when it is needed by you.

Inertia is a great thing, very common in the world you live in. Once you have reached the speed of your chosen route, you are unable to stop.

Thousands of crossroads fly past you, which will give you far greater opportunities than your miserable goal, but you, according to the rules of inertial motion, are carried along a pre-selected path.

You plan out your route: school, university, PhD, doctorate, chair, retirement, death - this is the route you will follow all your life.

The system offers you a rather limited number of routes at the beginning of your life, and you always have a lot of competitors on your chosen path.

Next to you, in this life, is a crowd of tourists just like you, limited in sense, rushing forward at a frantic pace.

And if someone in reflection tries to pause and ponder on the way, they are swept away by the general wave of those moving in the same direction.

And really, how can it be that the whole company is out of step and only one lieutenant is in step? It's not right.

Most people are quite satisfied with this offer. But only a small fraction manage to slip out of the general inertia.

That's us.

You want to know how?

Well, listen. Consider the humor to be over, the fairy tales too. Now the naked truth begins.

CONSCIOUSNESS

Human perception is primitive, miserable and limited. Yours, too, by the way.

The possibilities that lie within you are far greater than what you're realizing now. Far beyond that.

And it's not about the knowledge you have. You can be the most wonderful super-pu-per-professional, you can have many degrees and titles, as many top education levels as you want, but you are still primitive and limited.

Consciousness is like magic. Power (possibilities) and knowledge are gained gradually.

First you prepare the vessel and only then you fill it with water. So it is with consciousness. If the capacity of your vessel is small, then no matter how much knowledge you pour into it, only what can go in, will go in.

The consciousness of a human being is organized in such a way that its capacity is practically limitless. It is not without reason that we were created in the image and likeness.

But what would it be like if we all became like gods? Who would clean our divine latrines?

Ways to broaden the abilities of consciousness have always been the Holy Grail of all those on the path of magic.

We do not care much about gods at the moment. But the human body lives in human society and is therefore subject to all the constraints that society places on it.

All rulers in all times knew it as "Our Father" that it is much easier to control a person when his consciousness is loaded with standard programs.

It is easier and more pleasant to manage a standard person than someone who is aware of his individuality. It is true: you have to find a separate key to the personality, to individuality, to write a new counterprogram.

A standard person is wonderful because standard programs are quite suitable for him: all his buttons, hooks and strings are in their places, and their manipulation always gives, what is quite pleasant, a standard result.

Values, principles, shame or pride, morality - these are the means of manipulation that switch on the standard control emotions of fear and greed.

Society speaks to each of its members through these very mechanisms, forcing them to perform actions that will initially correspond to the values and principles embedded and inscribed within the consciousness.

Always and everywhere, in every era, in every religious or cultural system, society has regulated people's behavior through the fear to being expelled from that society.

Expulsion from the tribe guaranteed the outcast a quick

and qualitative death from cold, hunger or the teeth and claws of wild beasts. Expulsion from the religious community promised a rejection from all gods and deprivation of their powerful forces and supports. Excommunication guaranteed, at best, death at the stake after a not very pleasant series of tortures. Expulsion from the state meant at least the penitentiary and the same physical death for various reasons, but with an absolutely guaranteed result.

Fear is the basis of human control. Everywhere, all the time.

Fear of death, fear of losing property, fear of losing love, recognition, health - there are so many different fears in the human mind that it does not take long to find which button to press. Click at random, and you will almost always hit the top ten.

A formatted consciousness involves its division into many sectors and segments, some of which are filled with standard programs, while others are closed altogether, password protected and denied access.

Within the only working part of the consciousness, there are standard embedded programs that imply quite clear results in the external world. It is these programs that form the reality in which you supposedly exist.

The limited segment of your consciousness forms a similarly limited reality in your life, in which only the values and beliefs that are embedded in you from the beginning are able to work.

All children come into this world with a pure and unrestricted consciousness. But the moment when the cells of mom and dad come together, the rough and tough formatting begins.

By the time a person takes his first breath, his consciousness is already divided into segments. Programs are loaded into each selected segment, which people develop throughout their lives, mistakenly assuming that it is their full consciousness.

The last 700-800 years can be marked as the so-called realm of the mind, or realm of the Mental space, in a limited and controlled volume.

Some people have managed to keep open access to several segments of consciousness, either due to the ignorance of the controlling authorities or due to the connivance and negligence of the system. The society suppresses the attempts of such individuals to appear in the space of its influence in every possible way.

People with high sensitivity - they are also called psychics -able to read minds and influence the feelings of others at a distance, were locked away in asylums and out of sight.

People who are emotionally uncontrollable by the same society and have different desires are sent to places "not so far away"[6][7]

---

[6] *Places "not so far away"* is Russian slang for prison.

[7] or "very far away", depending on the severity of the discrepancy.

People with an ability to control the situation, and even more so those capable of sparking in others new values and life priorities were destroyed at once. Quickly and efficiently. To avoid unfavorable consequences, so to speak.

We have been killed, eliminated, burned at the stake, drowned, buried alive, beaten mercilessly, had complete collections of our own works burned on our backs, but we have come into this world again and again, because that is our mission.

And maybe yours, too.

Many of us have found a way that has enabled us to fully open our consciousness but remain invisible to those who have been destroying us ceaselessly.

You'll learn it too. Your journey will be shorter, but it will be no less painful. Because you will have to realize your own limitations, your own wretchedness, your own stupidity and your own emptiness. That is certain.

Your consciousness will have to be freed from its restraining elements gradually, slowly, step by step, expanding its possibilities until it understands itself.

With each round you will gain new knowledge and power. When a critical mass of power and knowledge is formed into experience, you will open the door to the hitherto closed off segment of your consciousness. You will feel empty and drained, but know that you have freed your consciousness from the material you have already worked through. Then you will start to accumulate power and knowledge again. The situation will repeat itself.

It will go on like this for quite some time, until that facet of consciousness that you have filled in loses the boundaries of reality and merges with you absolutely.

After that, you'll move on to the next round, and it'll repeat itself all over again.

Your body will be screaming, moaning, begging you to leave it alone. It is actually understandable - the enormous amount of energy you will use to do this will be disproportionately higher than what you would normally spend digesting a sandwich.

We don't know how long it will take you. But if you don't start now, you're at least one life too late.

When you are able to fill and open all your hitherto closed areas of consciousness this way, there will be an overall integration of body, consciousness, soul and mind.

By expanding your consciousness by microns, by grams - measure it in whatever you want - you will see and understand more.

You may need a mentor and a teacher at first, but not afterwards. You will be alone in your movement, but you will no longer feel any suffering or displeasure about it. You will be free of these human emotions and will be self-sufficient and fulfilled everywhere, in the crowd and in the desert.

First you will have a band of faithful companions walking beside you, then you will go in a caravan, then you will find only a few, and at some point you will realize that you're alone.

Then again there will be people, caravans and crowds, but they are no longer walking with you, but behind you.

And then you'll be alone again, and it'll happen all over again.

The process of acquiring force and knowledge is endless, just as life itself is endless, whether it takes place in this or in other worlds.

WORLDS AND REALITY

For most people, their world, their reality, is always the only one that exists.

It's not even the fact that many people are unable to travel a hundred kilometers from their homes and never go anywhere, and the world is known only through the TV screen.

It is not in physical movement that the meaning of comprehension of reality and the world is hidden.

The reality created by you and for you has nothing to do with traditional geography.

On this planet, on this Earth, there are thousands of different worlds living in parallel.

The term "parallel" was chosen to unify the understanding that there are worlds that are beyond our perception for the simple reason that parallel lines do not intersect.

You know this postulate from your geometry course at school, but it only applies when you are working on a 2D plane.

But if we take space, instead of 2D plane, our parallel lines will intersect.

It's just that most people do live on a 2D plane and are

doomed by it: time is judged by a calendar, age by the passport, life by a chain of events.

It's not their fault – they were painted that way.

But if you take your consciousness out of two-dimensional space, you will also have access to four-, eight- and sixteen-dimensional spaces, where the transition to parallel realities is quite easy.

Via their consciousness, mages are able to cross over to other dimensions, even in the physical body, and live there completely consciously.

It happens to you too. It is just that your formatted consciousness does not remember such transitions completely, because in order to reproduce them in your memory, all your spheres of consciousness must be open and the memory of "there" must be accumulated.

If the sectors that have been closed off so far are empty, there is no tool to preserve the memory. If an amoeba is moved from one Petri dish to another, nothing will change for it - it will not notice it.

But sometimes you have a vague idea that something wasn't quite right: like after a cloudy dream that left you with only emotional and bodily memories, but you can't remember the essence of it; or suddenly you "freeze up" and are carried away by your consciousness to an unknown place, and afterwards you can't reproduce anything in your memory either. Especially if your loved ones bring you out of the "freeze" with their natural "tactfulness" - with a kick in the arse, figuratively speaking.

Those who have managed - if not to destroy the boundary between the segments, then at least to thin it out, to poke holes in it - when reading fantasy and fiction, vaguely feel the reality of everything described there.

Goblins and elves, wizards and mages, dragons and witches - all these characters that they describe exist in reality. Only in another reality, not this one.

Traveling to other worlds is possible only under one condition - if one's consciousness is completely liberated and released from all constraining factors.[8]

As long as your consciousness is subject to a rigid format, as long as there is something in it that clings to you and keeps you firmly chained to the needs of your biology – you are a slave to that reality.

She will squeeze all the juices out of you, make you strive for someone else's goals, profess someone else's values, live a pre-scripted destiny.

The world of egregores is very cruel and jealous, it will never let you out of its clutches until you yourself demand it.

---

[8] Otherwise, the consequences for such a know-nothing mage can be catastrophic. Without getting rid of fears and hooks, his consciousness will become a space of entry to the inhabitants of other worlds. This is what happens to some unfortunate travelers (willing or unwilling - it does happen) when they return to find that they have changed dramatically. People around them no longer recognize them as their old acquaintances. They say: "It's like he's been replaced". Habits, emotions, reactions, even body shape change. An interdimensional traveler must be prepared to meet the natives, but under different conditions and different rules.

Have you seen The Matrix? It's very similar.

Only replace the world of machines with the world of egregores, and the fields where they grow humans inside the pods, with energy-informational consciousness of people; and it will become clear that the Matrix – the informational network in which the consciousness of each person is inserted into, exists in reality, but only in this reality.

Go beyond its limits and you are free. Learn to control this reality, understand the essence of its structure, and you are double as free.

REALITY

Egregores - the control structures - form major life concepts in people's perception, they paint a picture of the world.

The physically manifested world meanwhile remains unchanged - believe me, only someone who created it can change it. But the perception of this world is completely different in each person's consciousness.

Your attention will pick out of the world only those facts, qualities, events, that are presented in your inner world, in your mind.

Human consciousness is formatted in such a way that the sphere of perception of the surrounding reality includes only what is presented in the consciousness informationally. A family of elves may live near you, but you do not see them because you do not have the necessary information within your consciousness. Thousands of opportunities to fulfill your desire pass by you, but you simply do not pay attention to them, absorbed by the inertial motion in the 2D plane.

The reality created by you and for you is conditioned by the fact that you are part of the overall program and can only exist within that very program.

The informational space created by the controlling egregorial structures forces you to spend your power on creating other egregores within your own egregorial network, which only strengthens it.

You have achieved fame, popularity, honor and respect and have created your personal egregore. It fits into the general egregorial system and strengthens it.

Most people, seeing how you have achieved "success", fame and fortune, begin to aspire for the same. The system supports this aspiration in every possible way, pouring a flood of information on the immature minds of young or very young people.

Their consciousness gets filled with programs and information that make them completely forget about their true, personal, individual tasks.

The reality of each person is shaped by this informational current, which takes away the strength and energy of people who are included in it. They aim their desires towards the goals and objectives prescribed by the system.

Energy combines with information to form an energy-informational structure with rigid perceptual boundaries. It is these boundaries that do not allow you to see beyond your own nose.

You can see a large enough space with your eyes, but your consciousness will only see what is there informationally.

Once again, knowledge at the level of describing the world has absolutely nothing to do with it.

The crowds of tourists wandering around historical ruins

usually only check the box: I have been here, I have eaten here, I have seen this... But what have I seen? What have I experienced? In fact, having visited the ruins of several ancient civilizations, the average person will think that everything is the same, like in the supermarkets of the modern world....

Knowledge at the level of its perception by all spheres of consciousness - from feeling and sensation of the physical body to the awareness and "seeing" the informational currents running through it - speaks of the expansion of perception, and thus of the expansion of reality.

This selective perception of information gives our minds the illusion that this world is real.

ILLUSION

Illusion is like a fortress that every man builds around himself.

Its foundation is laid in the parental family, where the basic tenets of life in this world are explained.

Its further architecture is entirely the responsibility of man himself.

As soon as you said to yourself, "I'll never let that…" - you've erected a high wall around yourself that keeps the rest of the world out.

You say: "This is my principled position," and put up the second wall.

You say: "It's not for me," and the third wall is done.

You say: "I'll never understand this," and you shut yourself off completely.

In the course of life, people strengthen and ennoble the walls of their reality without even realizing that they have allowed themselves to have small, limited space for their possibilities.

They spend all their lives embellishing (or sugarcoating) this illusion they believe to be their reality.

Like magpies in their nest, they fill it with shiny things,

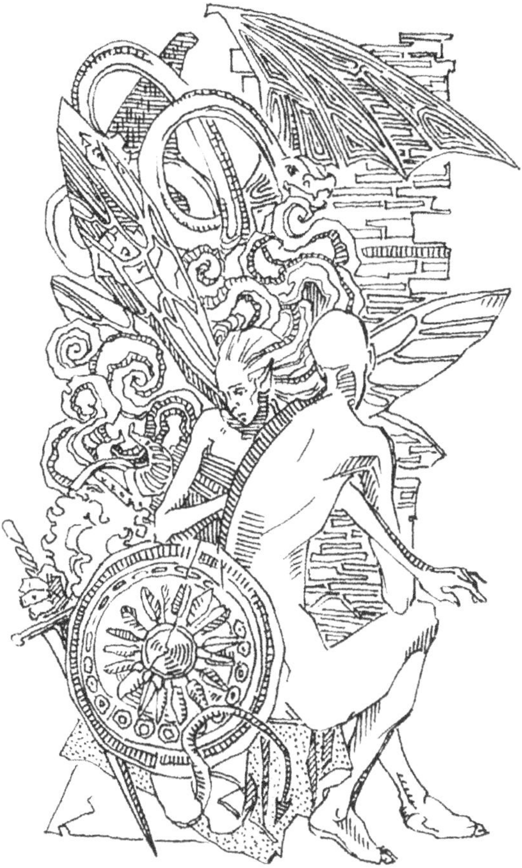

thinking that this is real wealth. They collect books and pamphlets, thinking that this is real knowledge; they try to drag other people into their nest too, thinking that that is love, friendship and good company.

The problem arises when you realize that your nearest and dearest person also has their own "tower of illusions", just like you. Only theirs is different for some reason.

And only when a bird suddenly flies over your head will you be surprised to think: "Where did it come from? " But people often manage to put a roof on top of it too, so that they don't even have to think about that.

This tower is your consciousness.

These walls that you put up on your own are rigid values and beliefs that the controlling system imposes on us.

All this imaginary comfort can be destroyed at any time. When the system is rebooted, illusions tend to dissipate. You are left alone with yourself, realizing that what made your life more or less meaningful is no longer there.

For a mage, it is an incredible luck, a breakthrough. For any other person, it is a catastrophe, a devastation, death.

But remember and never forget that living in an illusion is happiness for most people, for a few - a necessity. And for only a few, it is death.

If a mage is captured by illusion, it means a slow and sure death. He ceases to be a mage. Moreover, those who are fortunate enough to escape from the "tower of illusion" must start all over again in many ways.

Some of us, tempted by a comfortable and prosperous existence, have fallen into the net of illusion and become entangled in it.

People, existing in an illusory reality, live as if in a dream. Their day passes quickly and unnoticed. Their desires are limited to strengthening the walls and painting them in different colors (the most popular of them, for some reason, are pink and gray. However, there are some aesthetes who prefer stripes). Their lives are summarized in a few lines of the obituary.

If at some point you realize that you cannot remember what you did this morning or yesterday, if every day is similar to the previous one, it means that you are living in an illusion. Your program in which you are living has finished being built and you are locked in a tower.

If that is so, you have to dismantle these walls, brick by brick, from top to bottom. The illusion is an illusion, but coming into contact with a space free of illusion can simply crush your yet fragile consciousness. You may not be able to withstand this huge stream of signals from the outside world solely because all spheres of your consciousness are locked up, except for one. The one you are building your illusion around.

You take down and dismantle attitudes and principles very slowly and as you disassemble this tower, you begin to first see freedom, then breathe it, then hear it - and only then will you take a step away from the wreckage of the illusion. You will never do so if your intention to become a mage is not real, but merely inspired by fashion – another manifestation of illusion.

All of us have at some point gone through the journey of building this tower and destroying it, destroying our own illusions.

In order to complete this work, the mage would need his will in addition to the intention.

WILL

Will is the mage's purposeful and unchanging intention to achieve his goal - to obtain power and knowledge.

Will is all that remains of the mage, even when he has been captured by the illusion, even when his knowledge is lost and cannot be regained.

Will is the linchpin that allows us not to break down when we have to start over.

Will is what sets a mage apart from all others.

It is the quality of our power, its quintessence, which passes with us from incarnation to incarnation.

Combine the state of **"I Am As I Am"** with the intention to achieve the result, to achieve your goal. Listen to the sensations inside your consciousness. If at that moment you feel the boundaries of reality collapsing, as if they are sliding down from above, you are ready to begin.

But if the walls of the tower of illusions start to press down on you with redoubled force, if they squeeze your throat, keep on dismantling the walls. Your will is now paralyzed, immobilized. But remember, it is there.

When we have to rebuild ourselves from the ashes, from ruins, when we have to put our consciousness back together micron by micron, piece by piece, like the body of Osiris, it is our will that helps us to do it.

Will helps mages to walk their path. Will is able to change the course of fate's influence on the mage's path.

FATE.

You can safely divide all the people around you into two categories.

The first, think that everything is predetermined and nothing in life can be changed. All events, the whole life of these people is subject to written laws and following a preapproved script.

If you hear phrases like:
"That's my lot, I guess... "
"You can't escape your destiny…"
"To each his own…"
"Misfortunes never come singly…"
and other mental patterns of the same order, know that you are looking at a person from the first category. Let's call them "Fate-bearers".

The second category (much smaller, if not negligible, compared to the first) is of the opinion that man has free choice and free will always and in everything. Their position in life is characterized by the "strangeness" of their judgements and "strangeness" of their actions. Therefore, we will call them "Wanderers."

Basically, depending on which hypostasis a person accepts as dominant, that is the kind of life he lives.

The Fate-bearers have accepted absolutely and irrevocably the right to live inside the program. Remembering that the program works only within the created illusion (shell); they try their best to strengthen and confirm this illusion in every possible way.

Wanderers, on the other hand, do everything they can to go beyond the illusion and be outside the program. Without understanding why or what, they act in defiance of society, sometimes too aggressively for society to remain uninvolved.

Society, as you realize, is made up mostly of Fate-bearers. Wanderers are a thorn in their side. They're a pain in their neck. They're irritating. They simultaneously evoke in Fate-bearers the feelings of pity and a sense of inferiority[9].

From the point of view of the Fate-bearers, the life of the Wanderers is hard and unpleasant: they have no home, no land, no values, no authority - meaning, none of that that Fate-bearers usually have. Out of compassion (quite sincere, no doubt), they try their best to bring the lost sheep back into the fold, so to speak.

If a child Wanderer suddenly appears in a family of Fate bearers, it is trouble and grief for the parents. For the Wanderer, by the way, is no peach himself either. Endless conflicts, the issue of fathers and children, disownment – this is the least of what can happen with such an influence of the system.

The illusion in which Fate-bearers live determines their understanding and the construction of their own destiny. Those values they have defined for themselves will be the

---

[9] How can this even be combined?

basis of their movement through life.

If there is a belief that one must work long and hard to get results, their life will reflect that.

If they believe that everything is predestined from above, their will will be paralyzed, and there won't be enough strength even to have an intention to change life's course. Because the intention to do something is also something that is erased by the system. In order to avoid it, so to speak.

You may even meet people who can be characterized as "strong-willed" and "strong". The only problem is that their will and power are only strong enough to manifest these qualities exclusively within the framework of their own illusion.

Wanderers possess a will as is, with no obvious way for it to be practically applied by others. In other words, from the point of view of the Fate-bearers, Wanderers are people without will: wherever the wind blows, that's where they go.

This is the main characteristic of Wanderers - they do not stay long in any illusion. They are fascinated and interested in everything, but they do not stop at anything. From the point of view of the Fate-bearers, they cannot find their place in life.

The Fate bearers read horoscopes and go to fortune-tellers. They hate or despise their boss, not because he is an asshole or an absolute idiot, but because they depend on him. They follow the rules, but can't always explain why.

The Wanderers ignore all this, not in protest, but because they are not interested in living like that.

The Fate-bearers don't like Wanderers also because they vaguely assume that the fate of people "with oddities" is something strikingly different from their fate. It is perhaps more interesting, more fortunate.

However, they do not understand the main thing: Wanderers have no fate.

In order to become a mage, you have to be a Wanderer. In essence, by nature, by faith.

There is not a single Fate-bearer among us. When getting in touch with magic, Fate-bearers can become psychics, witches (and not bad ones, by the way). But never mages.

Anyone who allows the concept of "fate" to enter his life cannot be a mage.

A Wanderer is not necessarily a mage yet. But all mages are Wanderers.

For a mage, his movement towards his goal is a continuous road, a path to nowhere. And only the mage himself knows the direction of his movement.

Fate-bearers live in a world of illusion and depend on the plexuses of its web. They do not create informational processes, but only use them.

Some Fate-bearers are inquisitive enough to find an explanation for their inability to escape the enchanted circle of life (naturally, the explanation is provided while observing all the rules of formal logic). It was they who invented such concepts as fatalism and karma.

Invented, believed in, and reinforced the monolithic walls of their own illusion. Completely.

Any of their incarnation in this world goes according to the laws of karma, and their whole life depends on it.

KARMA

The term "karma" is often confused with "fate". It is believed to be an inevitable chain of events that leads to the same inevitable result.

As you realize, this is fundamentally wrong.

Fate is the manifestation of karma's action, but not karma itself.

Karma is primarily the law by which the life of any Fate-bearer develops. Meaning, it's that same program.

There may be prerequisites for an event in life, but the event never actually happens. Why?

Because only the Will can allow us to choose the one program that is right for each particular case out of many.

You don't get it, do you?

Well, look. You have a computer with a bunch of useful and useless programs in it. And the whole thing is called "software".

There may be programs that are necessary and unnecessary, application and system programs, they may be defective or corrupted by a virus. But they are just programs. Some are fast, others freeze all the time, some others come into conflict with other programs. But at the

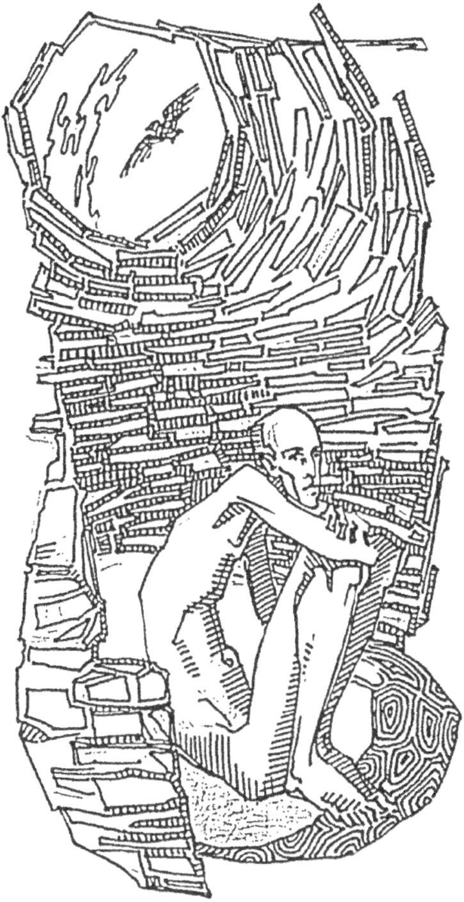

end of the day they are just programs.

The purpose of a program is to perform an action, to process and execute a command from above. The program always works for the result designed by its creator.

That's what karma is.

When a program unfolds "by default" it is a manifestation of karma's action.

The will of a mage (Wanderer, programmer) consists of not opening programs "by default", but only those that are needed; to delete unnecessary or impractical ones, and to install necessary and expedient ones. And doing it not just once in a lifetime (when you get so fed up that you can't go on), but regularly, according to your own tasks at hand.

A very exaggerated and simplified example, but it will help you to understand the interaction between Will and Inevitability.

All mages come into each incarnation with some karmic prerequisites. The task of each of us is as soon as you start to understand something, to make an inventory of all the programs embedded within you at birth.

Licensed software, copyrighted, no pirated versions, only the latest updates, and, as you understand, all with a lifetime guarantee. "Only the best", so to speak, from religion, nationality, democracy, capitalism-socialism - on point with brand, have no doubt about it.

This is the base version, so to speak. You can do the further configuration yourself, but the base version is what you have.

Why did you come into this life with particularly this base version? You'll find out when it's time for us to talk about death. Yes indeed, not birth, but death.

So, the first thing on the agenda is to get your base software in order. And of course, align it with your main goal, which is to accumulate power and knowledge. Once you've done that, you'll know exactly what to do with all the other apps, games and pictures.

Some people, born into the illusion of a certain family or nation (religion, political system - the only difference is the scale of influence) and having a good potential from birth, try to bring things in order - which is rightful and natural for everyone who has come here. But they do it for a goal prescribed in a specific program - the one in which they were born.

Meanwhile, the goal implanted into the consciousness by the system and manifested through the illusion of reality can vary: wealth, career, political influence, the Great American Dream or something simpler - a happy family life, house, household and other things related.

If at this stage you get caught in the illusion and assume the values of the system as your priority, you will be able to succeed within this illusion, and within this illusion only!

In doing so, unfortunately, you will get further and

further away from your true goal.

So, karma is, so to speak, a technical documentation of the program's activity, by which the informational network of your reality is built; your illusion, that is.

Karma manifests itself as a chain of cause and effect according to the principle either/or. Not clear again?

Like in a fairytale: the hero stands at crossroads, and there are three roads in front of him. In the middle there is a rock. On the rock there is an inscription: if you go left, you will lose your horse; if you go right, you will lose your wallet; if you go straight, you will lose your head. There is, however, a fourth way - back home, with your tail tucked between your legs.

That's a pretty clear prospect. Either way, it's inevitability, meaning fate.

But a Wanderer is already a mage in a way. A Wanderer goes destination unknown, but always knowing exactly why.

So, just as a man who follows the chosen path and gets the result written on the rock. A mage also goes, but the result is quite different: to beat the Nightingale the Robber, to fool Baba Yaga, to marry the daughter of the Prince of Kiev, and so on.

Russian fairytales allegorically depicted what a mage does. The Wanderer, who has a will and knows his goal, changes the laws of karma. Meaning, he gets a different result.

The principle of karma is a description of the operation of the system, a description of the operation of all this world's software.

Its peculiarity, we repeat, lies in the fact that it's laws operate only within the limits of the created illusion. If you leave the illusion, the laws cease to work, but only for you. Everyone walks this path alone, and your loved ones will remain where they were, you cannot force them out of the illusion.

But it is also not something people particularly desire. Remember, living in an illusion is good for many, very many.

They care about their illusion, they care about their reality. Don't ever try to convince anyone otherwise, knowing – keep quiet.

But since you have chosen this path by your will, the laws of illusion, the laws of karma must be known.

Someone who knows and has the power can predetermine the result and influence the outcome of events.

Karma is a multi-dimensional concept, and if you go beyond the usual flat thinking, you may be able to see that both time and events are intertwined within it.

It's a pretty extensive formula, but if you learn to manage your time, you'll also learn to influence the events.

Every person, absolutely everyone (and even more so a

mage), is upon birth given a so-called test program by the means of which he can correct the laws of karma in his life.

This program is called "a calling".

CALLING

It is wrong to assume that only a select few have a calling. Everyone has a calling.

It can manifest itself from birth, in which case you can say that you are lucky, especially if your inner circle is very supportive of your abilities and talents.

But calling can also come in a form that others do not see only because information about it is simply not present in their minds.

It is true that it is difficult to say that abilities and interest in blacksmithing, for example, is a calling. Although in the relatively recent past it was considered to be a special gift of gods.

A good voice is a talent, but how many talented singers do you know whose voice was able to incorporate such vibrations and sensations that your consciousness expanded to a volume unimaginable to yourself?

Managing people is a rare ability. Nowadays they teach all sorts of people to be "managers". But how often have you met a manager who does not have to tighten the screws, give slaps on the wrist or go to other unpopular measures to make his subordinates do something? A talented manager with a *Calling* is able to instill in the heads of his employees, without words and instructions, the tasks that they themselves are eager to fulfill. Have you met people like that?

People, for the most part, tend to do work that doesn't align with their interests.

They have neither the knowledge nor the will to see and implement their calling. Trapped in an illusion, they strive to achieve other people's goals and live according to other people's programs.

It is good if a person has a so-called hobby that he is able to pour his heart into and get a natural high from. But in this case, as a rule, he would *always* be met with condemnation from others, being laughed at and misunderstood.

You have experienced this attitude yourself. People in your inner circle roll their eyes if they see what literature you read, what music you listen to, what you devote every minute **of your** free time to. And that's at best.

In the worst case, there is fierce resistance, attempts to make you "fit in", to make you live "like everyone else". Sound familiar?

Of course it's familiar. All Wanderers sooner or later fall prey to rigid straightening attempts imposed by the system which tries to exert its influence on you via your environment, via society.

But it's very important, especially for someone on the path of magic, to find their calling.

It can be manifested in any form, but the main indicator of it is that you are attracted to it completely, regardless of external circumstances.

You realize that you can't NOT write.
You realize that you can't NOT communicate with people.
You realize that you can't NOT travel.
You realize you can't NOT dig in the dirt.
Can't not heal, can't not teach…

It is above you, it is stronger than you. The most important thing for any person, and even more so for a mage, is not to let oneself be overwhelmed by one's own calling and to develop one's abilities and talents, no matter what.

How does a mage's calling manifest itself?

A Wanderer by nature, by essence - it's always quite difficult for him to do one thing at a time. His abilities are enough to study for "good performance" grades, but his lack of desire to be liked prevents him from doing the same for "excellent performance" grades. His passions change frequently - he is interested in everything, and at the same time there is nothing that he is ready to commit to doing for the rest of his life. It's all from the point of view of others, of society, of the system.

But his hobbies, aspirations, ideas - they all are subordinated to a goal that is invisible to others. The mage acquires power and knowledge. He is in a perpetual search and in a perpetual motion.

Once he gets in touch with magic (and this can happen at the age of 5 or 55), he realizes what his way of all these victories and defeats was actually for.

Magic, as you remember, is first and foremost a system of knowledge. It can be applied in many different ways, from culinary arts to running the State as a system, from poetry to farming.

Calling is the wind. It always blows in the direction that will lead you to your true purpose.

A mage's consciousness is manifested through his talent for working with his own consciousness. He is able to dismantle his "tower of illusions", he is able to make a complete *upgrade* of the embedded and acquired software and without the slightest feeling of pity and self-humiliation to part with factors that allow the illusion to create his reality.

It is precisely through this "Calling" test-program that every mage is able to influence and manipulate karmic laws and create in his life the events that the mage himself needs in the "here and now".

EVENTS

Events take place in space and time. Every event that occurs, every event that is significant or not so much, has an effect on each successive event.

Events that possess a rigid, unchangeable sequence are called the karmic chain.

People are mostly familiar with the principles of building an event series, but this knowledge is purely intuitive and based on the principle of complete agreement. The Fate-bearers are resigned to their fate.

This humility allows them to see their lives only as a chain of events drawn out in the space of time's perception.

So, how are the events structured in space and time?

Events, as you realize, are directly related to karma, to the Causal[10] space. The action of karma is not random, everything has its preconditions and causes - it is programmed.

The boundaries of the illusion, manifested as rigid beliefs and values (the walls of the "tower of illusion"), define the shell of your life program.

The operation principle of this program (karma) forms

---

[10] Causal - relating to a cause. Not to be confused with casual - "accidental".

strictly specific events within the space of illusions, which are predetermined as the only ones possible within the framework of this program.

That is, an event can only unfold within the boundaries of a particular illusion.

The rigidity of Illusion's boundaries usually manifests itself in an absolute rejection of certain things.

What does it look like? It's very simple.

Absolute rejection of Pagan traditions, Judaism, Kabbalah, Christianity, etc. will not allow you the opportunity to study the many thousands of years of wisdom of these teachings and traditions, to apply the knowledge that you need now.

The belief "East or West, home is best" will prevent you from moving away from your home and not allowing events into your life that would be possible only if you are away from home (e.g. meeting a Voodoo mage or a Mexican witch – just to expand your horizons, nothing personal). On the other hand, such belief will direct all your attention into the space of your individual illusion and will guarantee a result within it.

Will the result satisfy your ambitions? That, unfortunately, is not guaranteed by the system. Its possibilities are not as limitless as many people think. On the contrary, they are very, very limited.

Where you told when you were a kid:
"Temper your ambitions"

"All covet, all lose"
"If you dance, you must pay the fiddler" - and stuff like that?
It's the system. It's the system trying to fit your desires to its capabilities.

If you ever agreed with it, you may now (as a result) suddenly start feeling rejection and denial. This is a signal that the system is beginning to rigidly format your consciousness, narrowing its boundaries.

By denying something, you put a hard wall between yourself and the rest of the world with all of its possibilities.

Opportunities imply the occurrence of events. The less restrictions you have, the more opportunities you are able to attract into your life. And later on, you can learn to shape them.

You can only attract what you already have - ready-made programs, ready-made events, ready-made situations.

Mages write their own program every time, and it's fast and unique. But they also use ready-made ones (why reject something that is available and functional?).

If a mage forms an event in the illusion of another person, he will naturally form it according to the laws that work in that illusion. Within karmic space, every event has a definite and guaranteed result!

Mages study and utilize the laws of the informational network of this world, since many of us live here permanently. And they interact with other people who do not even realize that they live inside the program.

Mages shape events themselves, knowing and maneuvering the karmic laws of this world.[11]

An event is the consequence of all previous actions (or inactions), manifested in time and space.

But neither we nor you have a need for random or sudden events. At the right time and in the right place - such a result is much more effective and necessary for the mage to form each following event.

Thus, in order for an event to occur, the following factors must be taken into account in the ritual of forming the event:
- the previous event series (the balance of forces at the time of the ritual);
- time factor;
- the location of the event occurrence in space (i.e. in which specific illusion the event is to take place).

The last element presupposes, of course, knowledge of the karmic laws of the illusion (reality) in which you form the event.

---

[11] Other worlds have other laws and a completely different principle of karma, i.e. informational support for the formation of events.

RITUAL

A sequence of actions for the purpose to achieve a result is usually called a ritual.

From generation to generation, knowledge of magical rituals is passed on by word of mouth or through written sources.

Many practitioners believe that possessing a description of a ritual will give them the ability to achieve a certain result.

This, unfortunately, is not entirely true.

Firstly, written sources never guarantee you a sure result. They only describe its probability.

Therefore, everything that will become your experience must be tested personally (!) in practice.

Secondly, a ritual only works for sure only when all its essential conditions are observed.

These essential conditions that are described in the ritual are usually masked by all sorts of nonsense, such as wailing, eye rolling and lots of unnecessary accompanying text.

That is why the rule for rituals, of any mage, so wonderfully formulated by Michelangelo di Lodovico di Lionardo di Buonarroti Simoni regarding marble work is:

"I just have to chisel away the superfluous material".

There's more unnecessary stuff in there than you think.

Such seemingly important things as ritual clothes, tools, favorable star alignment, etc., are only needed so a mage can enter the necessary state.[12]

But the main thing in a ritual is to recreate its essential conditions.

Essential is all that is necessary for the formation of the event (see above), because the purpose of the ritual is precisely the formation of an event.

And whether it happens right next to you or on the other side of the world depends only on the task that the mage is faced with.

Remember, that factors affecting the event must be considered without exception.

But note that all these conditions, especially the prior series of events as well as the time factor, are dynamic and subject to continuous change. This is why you will never be able to repeat the same ritual twice.

If the position of the stars changes, the result is changed.

---

[12] A state implies a stimulation of one's consciousness in such a way as to focus the energy of one's subtle bodies as much as possible and send it in the direction set by the mage. At all times, mages have used quite different means for this purpose: ecstasy, psychotropic or narcotic drugs, abstinence or, on the contrary, quality sex, starvation, self-torture, wearing chains, etc. Bringing oneself into a state of "holy rage" and drugging the mind with narcotics is certainly effective, but tends to wear out the body beyond repair.

Certain things happened between repetitions - and the final results are affected.

Last time you ate fish before the ritual and this time you have been fasting for a week, and this will affect the outcome of the ritual.

Besides, the mage who is performing a ritual, must necessarily be included into the informational system of the egregore the symbols of which he uses for his magical operation.

To do this, he must know the construction principles of that particular informational network, the laws by which it works, the values it implants in the minds of its adepts (at the expense of which it lives), and the consequences that are possible in this particular network.

Performing a demon-calling spell in Latin can only work in an illusion created by the Catholic sector of the Christian egregore (because "evil demons" are their parish). If you are not included in the informational grid of Catholicism, the ritual can have the exact opposite effect. That's the worst case scenario, the best case scenario is no effect at all.

In the same way, if you are plugging into a Pagan egregore, into the pantheon of Slavic gods or into the Kabbalistic structure of the tree of Sephirot, your consciousness must be included precisely in that corresponding egregore as informational structure.

Whether by bloodline, by religion, by previous

incarnation, you can use any connection that will help you in this endeavor.

It is difficult, of course, if you are a Protestant or Pagan by faith to learn how to enter, let's say, the Vatican's informational grid; but using the power of your bloodline can help.

BLOODLINE AND ANCESTRY

Every mortal man has ancestors, parents, and their blood lineage.

Your lineage is a unique combination of the genes of all your ancestors. Genes carry information. This information is a wealth of genetic wisdom.

Your biology is such that you got the strongest information from your parents (and they, in turn, from their parents).

To avoid any illusions, let's make it clear. Strong absolutely does not mean the best. It just means that it is most alive. Your ancestors who have lived in this world have passed on to you the strongest survival program.

In this program, in the genes, is the information of the biological species that your parents have managed to shape.

But if you are a mage, in addition to biological survival, you can also get information that is very important for you. A mage is, among other things, the guardian of knowledge that is present in the given bloodline.

You always have an unbreakable bond with your bloodline, with all its branches.

Once upon a time, consanguinity between the different branches was strictly prohibited. It was based on the power of the bloodline that a person was born into. But the Great Migration of Peoples has led to assimilation, and now you can find many very different strong and weak bloodline branches within you.

Like the roots of a tree, they nourish you with the life-giving juices of power, the power of your bloodline.

Power, as you remember, helps and facilitates the acquisition of knowledge. The stronger this connection with your roots, with your bloodline, the more force is in you.

The system prevents this in every possible way. In the end, people ended up becoming basically "like rolling stones, with no memory of their kinship". You may know your parents, and maybe their parents, but it is unlikely that you know all your ancestors 13 generations back.

But, you know, that's not a problem. Knowing with your mind is not the same as feeling. Knowing your ancestry, even the most detailed, will only tell you where to look. But what to look for? This is the most important knowledge in the search for the power of your bloodline.

How much different blood do you have in you? A lot, probably.

If so, you will have to make contact with every lineage, every tribe whose information is contained within your blood.

You must find power in each one of them, no matter

how difficult.

It's not easy. Bloodlines have been in conflict, many tribes have been in constant enmity with each other, and this information is also in your genes. So one bloodline can make you stronger and another can make you weaker, putting you at conflict with your essence for reasons you don't understand.

This is why the joining of a man and a woman from different tribes and bloodlines has always been met with fierce resistance from the clan elders and the Blood Guardians. Later on, a rather clever solution was found: the man or woman "converted" to the faith of his or her loved one or took a new name.

Those who converted to another faith symbolically renounced their connection with their bloodline, their ancestors and their informational influence on their lives.

But, as you realize, this connection cannot be broken, it is preserved in your genes. You yourself can make this connection manifest in your consciousness. So that this force, this power of your ancestors, is directed towards your main goal - to acquire and accumulate power and knowledge.

Information, passed on to you in coded form by your ancestors, is the connection between you and the informational structure, the egregore of your bloodline - your tribe.

Even without knowing exactly what blood mix is in you, you can feel these connections, sense them in yourself.

You can awaken the power that your forefathers have been gathering bit by bit and saving for thousands of years.

Just don't mislead yourself with the illusion that belonging to a certain bloodline is as good as written in your passport. There are more branches within you than you realize.

In the case of aggressive chauvinism, rejection of this or that blood or origin - this is how your genetic memory manifests in the present incarnation. What is the reason for this enmity, this rejection? You can remember this information if you manage to awaken the memory of your ancestors.

But for a mage, the reasons for the past enmity of his ancestors is just information that he can use for his own purposes. But it is not the purpose itself.

If a mage becomes involved in an old feud, if he allows this information to take over his consciousness, it will bring about terrible consequences. The world of this reality uses this information, fueling with it such instruments of control as national strife, religious wars, economic conflicts and other tools that are meant to control people's consciousnesses.

This is how a mage can become a weapon of the system.

If you sometimes find yourself disliking Blacks, Whites, Jews, Russians, Americans, Christians, Jews, damned Pagans and the like, know that it's not you, it's the system. Ask yourself a simple question: "Who benefits from it?"

and if the familiar feeling of a hoop around your head reappears, you've come to the right conclusion.

Mages do not allow their force to be used by the system. Mages use the system themselves. This is not war nor hostility. Mages don't engage in war.

The world of this reality is the world of manifested illusions. Therefore, it is not the most convenient informational system for a mage, however, it is needed by this world. If it wasn't there, the universal balance of all informational systems of other "parallel worlds" would be disturbed. All worlds must live in harmony, and no one can dominate within this information system.

The task of mages is to preserve universal balance. And here, mages fulfill an important mission: to keep the system within the limits. But remember: although this is the mage's task, it is not the goal. The task helps to achieve the goal, but does not replace it.

The information that is contained within your bloodline is aimed specifically at fulfilling this mission, at solving an important task.

If you get out of your still very limited head the idea that some knowledge has certain exclusive truth to it and similar nonsense, you will surely be able to notice one quite obvious thing. All religious teachings (not to be confused with religion as part of the system) are essentially talking about the same thing.

In allegorical and figurative form, they describe to the mage the principle of this world's mechanism, showing

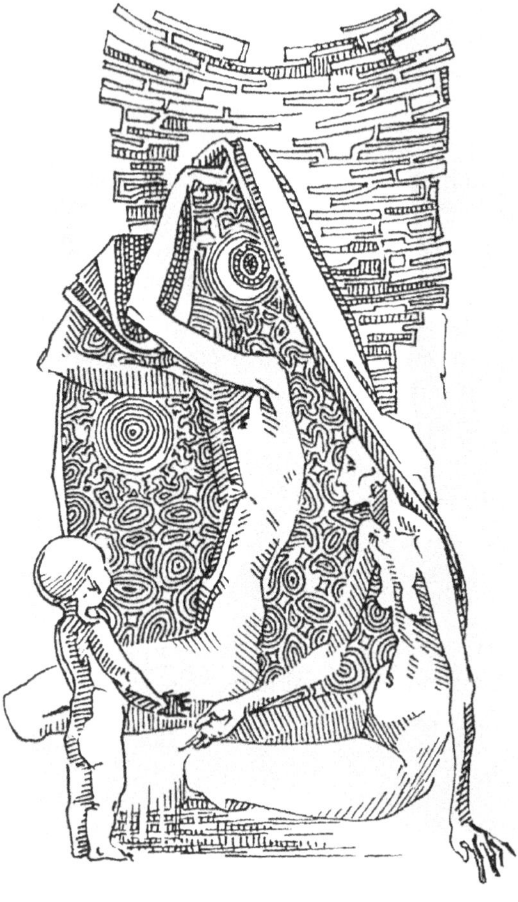

him where there are weaknesses, and teaching him how to control this system.

Why was this particular presentation form chosen? The Gospels, the Bible, the Kabbalah, the Vedas and other apocrypha of antiquity can be read correctly only by people with an open mind, who can instantly unpack all the symbols encoded in them. That is, by the mages.

Opening your ancestral force channel can help you not only gaining an additional source of power, it can also help you to *correctly* understand the message of your blood lineage.

Now you can understand why some sources awaken in you a hitherto unknown sensation of touching the sacred, while others seem completely empty.

A great number of esoteric informational sources send people in search for magical knowledge along a confusing and long path. The interest in Satanism, Shamanism, spiritualism, occultism and other "isms" was for many Wanderers just a tribute to fashion and had nothing to do with the ancestral source of knowledge.

Sure, you can go to Altai shamans or to Don Juan in Mexico in search of knowledge, but if you cannot bloodline-wise integrate yourself into the informational system of another nation, you will have to undergo a difficult and painful initiation.

It is painful also because you have to close your innate bloodline channels that have nourished and sustained you all this time, even if you didn't really notice them.

A descendant of the Drevlians or Kriviches will never be able to understand the secrets of African Voodoo magic, even if he lives in a tribe of that culture all his life. Some mages do, however, get access to other information, but how and why - you will find out further on.

Open in yourself this powerful informational channel of your ancestors. Accept them in yourself, do not deny it.

For if you close your eyes on the 1/64th Jewish (or Buryat, Tatar, Mongol, Gothic, etc.) blood in you, you may lose the opportunities of acquiring knowledge given to you from birth.

The knowledge that you have brought from past incarnations, merged with the knowledge of your ancestors, will strengthen you many-fold.

Let this force awaken in you, do not deny it. The knowledge that you receive through this source of information will land into your individual storehouse of knowledge that no one can take away from you.

Why is it that some people are able to preserve and unpack the archaic information of the bloodline and their past incarnations, while others are not?

To answer this question, we need to consider the developmental process of the human consciousness.

But not from the moment of birth, but from the moment of death.

DEATH

The thing people fear most in the world is the unknown. Death is the most unknown thing the human has in terms of his sense of the unknown in general.

No one has ever returned from there and no one has ever been interviewed on television about it. The few sources that describe "life after death" experiences are regarded by official science as the results of some altered states of consciousness due to a lack of some hormones in the brain. Live with this explanation, dear citizens.

People who have not only touched death, but have experienced it, generally have no need of "sharing" that kind of information.

Death is a great and solemn transition from one world to another.

Different cultures in this world have very different attitudes towards death. For some, it is grief; for others, it is undeniable joy.

People only grieve for those who have left because they themselves have remained here. Remember the traditional wailing "What will I do without you?!" - and it will immediately become clear that people do not cry as much for the departed, as much as for themselves.

Those nations who are convinced that "it is better over there" have no sense of grief and loss in their culture nor consciousness, but rather the joy of liberation.

For the average person, the thought of death usually means the loss of everything, or nothingness. This attitude is derivative of the same illusion about oneself and one's own life.

What happens to a person's consciousness when it is time for them to touch death?

Terminating a life program is very similar to transferring data from one computer to another.

When your computer becomes obsolete, you first try to make it work better, i.e. you treat your body and try to prolong its active existence. When it (the computer or the body) breaks down completely, you take all the data you **need** and transfer it to another medium.

At the moment of this transfer, you get rid of information that is unnecessary, but leave all the important information.

Whatever you identify as important, you will carry forward!

The same thing happens with the human consciousness. If due to the limitedness of your own consciousness and absolute involvement in the illusory reality you did not have time (did not want) to make a copy of all your achievements on an external medium, it vanishes along with your old body. The important data is recorded in the form of an informational structure and provides a starting platform for a new incarnation.

Because the memories of an ordinary person are tied to the energy inherent in a particular physical body (which now is different due to the new incarnation), it is impossible to reproduce the experience of a previous incarnation.

And so man suffers, and in memory of his ancestors laments the fate that brought him to these boondocks and dropped him at the bottom of life. Or, on the contrary, he thanks all the gods (which happens much less often) for the good fortune of being born there and being who he is...

But that's just half the battle.

It is always possible to start from scratch - many of us have done just that. If a mage, due to circumstances, has not been able to retain his memory in full, then, even without realizing his calling, he will subconsciously still look for an opportunity, for a thread that will bring back this memory.

The ways can be very different: psychology and extreme sports, philosophy and chemistry, esotericism and martial arts... - all of these are attempts to reach, to grasp the obscure that doesn't let the mind find rest.

But what is to be done if you have no such opportunity, if your karma is such that it does not give you a choice? In order to answer this question, one has to deal with the causes.

The key lies in the past. The incarnations you have had before have largely determined the foundation for the "base software".

As you already know, when the life program starts to wind down, the information of your individuality begins to get condensed and archived.

Then, having passed through all levels of consciousness and transformed into information, it must get to the common informational space (Atman). To get realized and transformed there means the purification of the **monad**.

But living in an illusion and belonging to a certain egregore does not allow it to do so. Your program gets stuck in the egregorial space, and its disembodiment does not take place.

Your informational structure remains in the space of ideas you have served all your life. The energy and information of the egregore reinforces the karmic preconditions, binding you even more to the part of the web in which you are entangled.

This is exactly what Jesus Christ (the Messiah) said in his commandments - "Thou shalt not make any graven image."[13]

One's belonging to a certain informational structure leads to the fact that in the next incarnation he will come with certain life prerequisites: body, social environment, opportunities, era... No choice.

---

[13] Graven image - idol, mental image, representation.

Remember Jesus' words: "It is easier for a camel to go through the eye of a needle than for a rich man to enter the kingdom of heaven". If you understand the true meaning of these words, you can understand *exactly what* Jesus was talking about in his proverbs. The rich man has on his mind the multiplication and preservation of wealth; all his desires and intentions are directed towards this goal.

Ask any man with money (with good money!) and he'll tell you that making many is not the hard part; the hard part is to save it.

By saving, however, you do whatever it takes, which subordinates you to that very goal - preserving wealth by any means necessary.

This is exactly what the Messiah meant when he said: "You cannot serve both God and Mammon."[14]

It is not about the incompatibility of wealth with spiritual growth. It is about the substitution of goals. To "serve" is to belong entirely to the one whom one serves.

The kingdom of heaven, paradise, is the informational space where a complete liberation from all karmic programs and knots can take place.

If your consciousness during your lifetime was completely included in the ideals and values prescribed by the illusion, then, upon coming to a new incarnation, you will be forced to receive these very values as the main

---

[14] Mammon (mamona) - God of wealth; worldly goods.

basic (karmic) programs.

If you were attached to the values of wealth - you are to be born into a poor family or be an artist in a family of financiers. If you aspired to fame and prestige, all the prerequisites of the present incarnation will be such that you will have neither.

Note that wealth, fame, and prestige in past incarnations are not as important as your ardent striving for it. Even if these aspirations did not lead you to your cherished goal, you will still strive for the same heights with a tenacity worthy of a donkey.

But that's not even the point. The main thing is that you will have to suffer for lacking whatever it is that you are striving for. You will be forced to pursue these illusory values at all costs.

By realizing this mechanism, you will be able to avoid dependence, correct the influence of the preconditions of previous incarnations on your present life now, and free your future from certainty.

But only if you are free from any attachments, only if passions are not tearing your consciousness apart.

You already know what mages do with the information of their own consciousness. It is very important to keep the important information on an external medium until you get a new body, and until the capabilities of your new consciousness allow you to unpack it in full and without distortion.

As you realize, only a few can do this, and we have spent thousands of years building up expertise in this skill.

You're luckier than we are. You can get this knowledge in a much shorter time. Because now there is an algorithm, and this algorithm is ready for transfer.

Now, our capabilities are much greater than they used to be. A couple of centuries ago, we had to look for someone who could tell us where to look for, or to give a hint.

But in this informational system, despite all the rigidity of its influence on people's minds, there is something that is a unique tool for working with the consciousness and one's memory.

That tool is the word.

WORD

The informational system in which you live has complete control over your values and beliefs. It influences all events that take place in your reality. The only thing left to a person is he himself AS IS, and his thoughts.

The Mental space is relatively free and accessible compared to other informational layers of consciousness. Therefore, people of this world have done their best to perfect this part of their consciousness.

Thoughts are a means of communication of the person with his own self. But people can communicate their thoughts to others only through words.

Your consciousness is capable of working in completely different ranges of perception of information, but the rigid formatting you already know about has limited not only your memory, but also your ability to expand it.

Living in the sphere of influence of the illusory world, you can only perceive and transmit information through words.

You think telepathy is impossible? It's only impossible in this world.

Telepathy - the transmission of thoughts over distance – is only possible under the condition of a free space. In a world of illusions, any thought will become entangled in a web of information, in a mesh of concepts from which people build the towers of their personal realities.

This web is everywhere, and the low-powered signal you transmit in a form of thought, is simply dissolved by the influence of the system's resistance.

All people of this world have tremendous telepathic abilities. All without exception. But only mages are able to rise above the sphere of illusion and direct their consciousness into the open space.

The average person who enters another world, such as the world of Air or Water, is surprised by his ability to communicate with other inhabitants of this world without the aid of words and to move instantly over long distances.

But in the world of manifested illusions everything is different. For a thought to overcome space and time, it must overcome the resistance of the web, overcome the distortions and noises of space. For this to happen, a powerful energetic message is necessary. None of the people know how to accumulate energy this way and direct it through a constructed ("allocated") channel. Mages can do it.

But in order to communicate with each other, we don't need to waste our power on a simple "hello", overcoming the resistance of the web of this world. It is enough, as it has already been said, to just take your consciousness outside its influence.

But to get the message across to the man of the illusionary world, we must use the tools that are familiar to him.

That tool is the word.

Because it is precisely your Mental sphere that they've helped you to develop since infancy, all your other abilities are most likely present in a latent, dormant state. This has created a serious bias in the sphere of informational perception - as a rule, the ordinary person is not able to perceive information consciously, neither through feelings nor through *sensations*.

Word is his only tool.

But words and even sounds have a tremendous impact on a person of this world. The word not only carries information, but it can influence the subconscious in a completely unexpected way.

The word can open up your hitherto unexplored capabilities. But it can also close them down forever.

Consciousness of people is encoded by the system from the beginning, but it's also true that you can find codes and keys to your own subconscious reserves through the same element - the word.

In the world of illusions, anything that has to do with spells and enchantments has been considered forbidden for over a thousand years. Do you ever wonder why?

Right, because open access to the ancient knowledge

about the influence of words on the human subconscious is not favorable to the system, especially if it is used by all and sundry.

In the past, people who knew the power of the word were ruthlessly dealt with by the system - to the stake or to the chopping block (your choice). Nowadays, these methods are not popular any longer, but even now, the public chastising, accusations of charlatanism or fraud are in fact no better.

The power of the word cannot be overestimated. It has a tremendous impact in this very world.

This is why the Mental space is honed here as nowhere else. And that is why there are things here that can't be found practically in any other worlds.

It is the greatest miracle, the greatest good - and a terrible weapon. It's literature.

LITERATURE

There is no other way for people who are born and living in this world to communicate with each other except through the Mental realm. Literature emerged as the quintessence of all the capabilities of the Mental plane. It was through literature that people were able to convey not only their thoughts but also feelings; not only feelings but also ideas; not only ideas but also values.

Realizing the power of literature, the system has at all times tried to regulate this source of information, allowing and not allowing, diluting and embedding, prohibiting and permitting.

But the power of words and the capabilities of literature give you and your fellow Wanderers the right to get the information they need.

When printing was not yet developed, we used to preserve information via written medium, but rarely. Back then, we more often preserved and passed on our innermost knowledge and acquired skills by the word of mouth, from teacher to student.

But as times went on, and with each passing day the capabilities of the word became greater, the development of literature and the progress of consciousness could no longer be held back. Literature inevitably poured into our lives.

Thought began to spread faster than the speed of light.

In no other world is literature as advanced as in this one. There is no way to overestimate its power.

Once the system realized that it was no longer possible to contain thought and literature, it adopted a method which almost destroyed this wonderful and beautiful offspring of the human mind. It decided to crush the word with printed volume.

What does it look like? Very simple. For one thought, for one book that is capable of freeing a person's consciousness from the web that is holding it back, it produces a hundred more volumes aimed, as you realize, at achieving the exact opposite.

You may have noticed that when you read books on a topic of your interest, such as esoteric knowledge, development of consciousness, theosophy, for example, that at some point you realize that you have already read it before, that it has been written already. The works repeat each other like clones. But there is a difference between a living thought and its clone.

The living word reveals a huge number of sensations, emotions, and intuitive ideas in your mind. A cloned word is empty, there is nothing in it. Cloned books are characterized by their emptiness.

A distinctive feature of cloned literature is that a thought, when it comes into contact with it, seems to get as if bogged down, you cannot trace it. It's as if your consciousness freezes up, deprived of feelings and sensations. This is how the system's books work. Their main task is to stop the thought.

The living word, living literature awakens thought and opens the senses. In an attempt to save the living word, man invented a wide variety of genres, and the most successful of them: fantasy, science fiction, fairy tales - have proved to be especially resilient and were able to penetrate everything and everywhere. They did not seem to be something serious to the system - fairy tales and fables, nothing special.

But through these fairy tales, the living word managed to penetrate people's minds, allowing them to ponder, allowing them to dream.

You will have to learn how to distinguish a living word from a cloned word. To do this, you will have to dig through an enormous amount of various literature until your eyes ache, until they cramp, until they hurt. But this will help you to learn through practice, to tell from the very moment you are picking up a book, to recognize from the very first lines what kind of book it is, whether it contains a living word.

You will learn to separate the grain from the chaff, you will be able to tell empty rubbish that you have been slipped under the guise of a "terribly ancient grimoire" or "extremely advanced literature" from truly unique knowledge.

But you can only achieve this skill through practice. Do not Spare you time - you are gaining knowledge and experience. This is an important, very important step on your path to becoming a mage.

Implicitly, you will learn *to read*. You think that you can read? Don't be ridiculous. You're educated in literacy, which, let's face it, is not the same thing.

To read, for a mage, is to see the true meaning in everything, whether explicit or implicit.

To read is to be able to unpack each Word automatically in your consciousness; to recognize both its informational affiliation and its potential to influence subconscious processes.

A mage can instantly detect the encoding system through written words, thereby quickly distinguishing cloned literature from living literature.

Word and literature are universal tools that help not only the mage but also the ordinary person to control the influence of the system on his or her consciousness.

You just must learn *to read*.

WORLD OF ILLUSIONS

It is time for us to talk about this world.

You have already realized that any world is governed by the informational system represented in it. But who created this system, where did it come from?

Lately it has been quite common to hear from some Wanderers that certain "other-planetary beings" are to blame for everything. The Fate-bearers prefer a "Jewish Masonic conspiracy" theory.

The theories are good, why bash them? They are.

Trying to find an external enemy is always very convenient because it completely removes the responsibility from the individual.

But we have to disappoint you. Neither aliens, nor the Jews, nor the Freemasons, nor other "great and terrible ones" have anything to do with it.

The world of illusion is the creation of human beings. And it is not somewhere out there. It is inside every head.

Throughout humanity's development, human beings have espoused values and beliefs that are derived from human passions such as greed, avarice, pride and fear. In an attempt to justify these very human vices, people have created an entire philosophy, a system of concepts and explanations that have slowly but surely replaced the true

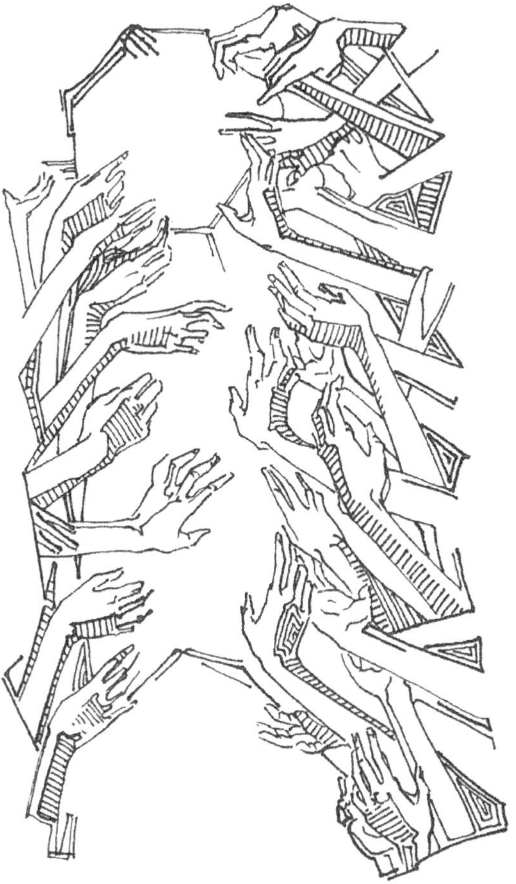

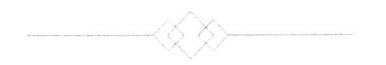

values of the human person as an individual.

It did not start yesterday, but many thousands of years ago. Slowly but surely people created an informational system of collective reason, which began to control them.

People gave a great deal of energy to this space, forming collective, shared values that justified their desire to fulfill their most simple needs.

The informational control system - the system of egregorial structures - is a web that a spider weaves for the purpose of hunting.

Have you ever seen a fly caught in a spider's web? Do you understand its features? That's right, the more you wiggle, the more you get caught and tangled.

It is the same in this system - the more you resist, the deeper you are sucked in by the values of the illusory world. The energy you put into the struggle will be swallowed and digested by the egregorial systems and the whole informational structure. It does not care whether you send it a positive emotion or a negative one. There is no difference, it is omnivorous.

The more energy you give, the more the system sucks you in; the values and principles that the system instills in people's consciousness leave them completely shackled and bound.

The only way, as you realize, to preserve yourself and your freedom is to relax.

The main value that the system instills, is to rise above others. The great American dream is that in the country of United States of America, everyone has equal opportunity, regardless of starting conditions, skin color or mental ability, and anyone can easily become a President. The slogan of the young Soviet Republic, that a cook can run the state, is a derivative of the same idea.

"Fight for power," says the system, "fight for fame, success and wealth! Put all your power, all your energy into it! You have many competitors, so cheat, kill, burn, destroy dissent with fire and sword – do whatever you think is necessary if it shall bring you closer to your goal!"

The poor human creature, not yet having sorted out his life's purpose due to juvenility, receives this value ready-made, with all the instructions and justifications.

The system will catch you in its net if you *really* want fame and wealth, power and honor. In this case, you will be forced to use the mechanisms and methods prescribed by the system to achieve this goal (someone else's goal, mind you!).

To want without wanting, to wish without wishing - remember we talked about this at the beginning? It's an opportunity to free yourself from the sticky threads of the spider's world. It is a great art and skill that you will have to learn - to never let your desires and passions consume you completely.

This informational system was created by people. It cannot exist without them, and they depend on it.

In this world, people have values and beliefs created by an informational system that they themselves have created. But the single law of all worlds is quite simple and unambiguous: "You made it, you take it apart."

Therefore, it is useless to cry out to God complaining about your failed life. God will not interfere with what people themselves have created. That is the law.

SAVIORS AND PROPHETS

Periodically, there are mages who come to this world trying to save it from destruction.

They awaken others via the word – the only instrument available to human consciousness – the understanding and principles of saving men from themselves.

Through the word, all the prophets who came to this Earth tried to convey to people the only possible way - find your fulfillment.

Do everything you can for your consciousness, don't expect help from anywhere. Help is always a crutch, always a deception.

Christ in his parables and deeds, whether explicitly or implicitly, freed people from crutches; Allah and Mohammed (his prophet) and even Buddha said the same thing.

The teacher's arrival meant a salvation and awakening for many of us. But the system was not slumbering.

Religion was turned into a doctrine, and by means of it they began to destroy those who thought differently.

Thus, the teaching ruined itself without ever achieving its goal.

Whoever wishes to follow the path of magic must be

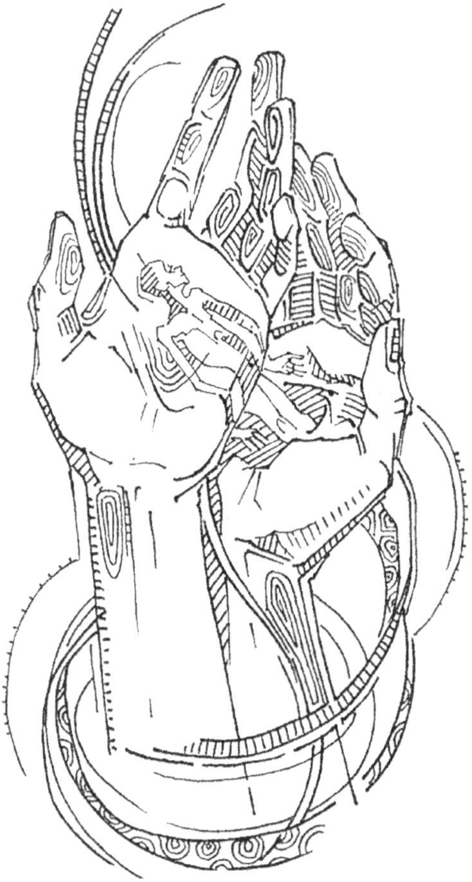

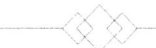

prepared for the fact that nothing will happen by itself. Knowledge will not be given ready-made – everything must be sought; everything must be achieved. On your own.

Even if you have the right to magic by blood, the system will do everything possible to ensure that this right is never realized. The system has no need for surprises. And a mage is always someone who cannot be calculated by the system.

This book is the first in the volume of information that will follow. The system is killing us with our own weapons, and you already know how it is doing it.

So from now on, filter all information, let it pass through you, through your consciousness, through your essence **"I Am As I Am"**.

This will help you to free your consciousness, expand and integrate your power and accumulated knowledge in the shortest possible time.

This will make you immune to any egregorial influence, you will be able to rise to the above-eggregorial space – just where the consciousness of those who work for magic exists.

HOW TO LEARN

All the knowledge of this world lies in the depths of the centuries. It's in history. It's in mythology and legends. It is in the knowledge of mythology and in the understanding of the functioning of various gods and pantheons.

Gods are not the imaginations of the uneducated masses. Gods are real. It's just that their image is not human; their reasoning is completely different from that of Homo Sapiens. If we see gods as human beings and evaluate their families by the same standards as our own family, misunderstanding and mistakes are inevitable.

Gods are not human beings. Gods are conglomerates of information, their minds are the sizes of planets and the Universe. It is impossible to understand it with the human mind. But you can try to awaken the memory of them in your consciousness and through this connect with them. Find the access keys and thereby establish an unbreakable link with your gods. To change under the influence of their forces, to learn from them, to develop under their control.

But in order for the simplest human mind to be able to assimilate the complex informational flow of his deity, he must constantly change his consciousness, constantly expand its frequency capacity range.

It takes practice to do that.

The methodology I practice among my students gives positive results. It combines both theory and practice, evenly and purposefully expanding the consciousness of those who receive the formation.

Briefly, the method is as follows:
1. Development of the consciousness by bodies (The Main Department) - the subconscious, the Mental plane, the supraconscious (sequentially). The method provides an opportunity to develop the ability of the mind to perceive more and more energy and information with each step.

2. The General Theory of Magic is a parallel course. This is the study of ancient myths and legends and the ability to decipher messages embedded in them. My students form their own magic system based on these messages.

3. In addition - the ability to work with the Elements as the most important energetic resource of this world. What we have here is rather painstaking work based on the ancient practices of the Druids: the ability to feel the Elements, the ability to see the manifestation of the Elements, the ability to receive the effects of this manifestation, the ability to influence the Elements and change their manifestation. Also in this course - the basics of healing.

4. Additionally - the Rune course, which includes comprehension of runes, connection of one's own consciousness to the informational database by the means of runes, the ability to use runic

formulas and to compose them, the ability to work on the channel of gods of the Norse Tradition.

5. Additionally - the Tarot course, which, being a magical catalyst, accelerates the evolution of consciousness, triggers the process of transformation of human consciousness into the consciousness of a mage.

6. And something else. From the witchcraft section, something secret/practical.

If you are going to study on your own, I recommend you follow this algorithm - first prepare your consciousness on the 1st, 2nd and 3rd circle and only then take information through a mythological source. For all the seeming "nonseriousness" of legends and fairy tales, they tend to powerfully turn one's consciousness inside out. And if the mind is not ready for such a transformation, it can have extremely negative consequences.

By now, several books have been written to help people like you. From me to you. Here they are:

1. **'The intricacies of Fate, or What Dimension you Live in?'** Textbook on working with the Etheric body. Development of sensations and the base state "I Am". Dimensions of reality and how to determine "What level is your consciousness stuck on". Methods of initial self-change. *The method of entering the 1st Circle.*

2. **'The Subconscious is Omnipotent, or Controlling the Energy of Your Desires'** Textbook on working with the Astral body. Getting rid of fears and negative consequences of the past. Emotion control methods. *The method of entering the 2nd Circle.*

3. **'Controlling the Energy of Your Thought'** Textbook on working with the Mental body. Controlling the realm of goals. Controlling the word. *The Method of entering the 3rd Circle.*

4. **'Karma – the Law of Cause and Effect'** Textbook on working with the Causal body. Control of events and formation of cause-and-effect relationships. *The beginning of magical transformation.*

5. **'Runes Reveal the Mysteries of the World'** A complete textbook on runes. *Magical Craftsmanship.*

6. **'The Power of the Bloodline - a Woman's Mystery'** A textbook for unlocking the power of the bloodline. Rules of distribution of rights within the bloodline. *Recommended predominantly for women-witches.*

7. **'True Woman'** A textbook of consciousness transformation includes practices designed for 1 year and 1 day. *Recommended predominantly for women-witches.*

8. **'The Key to Knowing Yourself'** Textbook for identifying specific features of your consciousness: energy exchange preference and psychotype. These indicators determine the further specialization. *Recommended for all those involved in the practice of magic.*

The library on my website also has a large collection of literature about magic intended for mages, both beginners and seasoned practitioners.

As well as the necessary video and audio seminars for effective training.

I would be happy if the methodology I use to teach my students could help you too.

For more information about my School, follow the QR code.

With honor,
Menshikova

Made in United States
Orlando, FL
24 February 2025

58846709R10089